P9-CTQ-708

OCCUPIED
TERRITORY

Other Books by Cal Thomas:

A Freedom Dream, 1976

Public Persons and Private Lives, 1979

Book Burning, 1983

Liberals for Lunch, 1985

with Dr. Ralph W. Neighbor, Jr.

Target Group Evangelism, 1975

OCCUPIED TERRITORY

Cal Thomas

WITHDRAWN
HILLSDALE COLLEGE
LIBRARY

Wolgemuth & Hyatt, Publishers, Inc.
Brentwood, Tennessee

MICHAEL ALEX MOSSEY LIBRARY
HILLSDALE COLLEGE
HILLSDALE, MI 49242

PN
4874
.T418
A25
1987
c.2

© 1987 by Los Angeles Times Syndicate and Cal Thomas.
All rights reserved. Published September, 1987. First Edition.

No part of this publication may be reproduced, stored in a
retrieval system, or transmitted in any form by any means,
electronic, mechanical, photocopy, recording, or otherwise,
without the prior, written permission of the publisher, except
for brief quotations in critical reviews or articles.

Published by Wolgemuth & Hyatt, Publishers, Inc.
P.O. Box 1941, Brentwood, Tennessee 37027.

Printed in the United States of America.

ISBN 0-943497-02-7

gift
3/21/97

To Ray Miller

CONTENTS

ACKNOWLEDGEMENTS

It is possible to fail on your own, but no one succeeds in a vacuum. He or she is always influenced by others.

While I am grateful to many for serving as role models and mentors in my life, one man provided more than an example for me to follow. He gave me a standard of excellence by which all journalism ought to be measured.

He is Ray Miller. This book is dedicated to him because much of what I have been able to achieve has been the result of what he taught me, the encouragement he gave me, and the trust he placed in me during the formative years of my career.

Ray Miller was properly cited by the National Press Photographer's Association in 1981 for establishing a standard of excellence in photo journalism. He is also the winner of a Peabody Award for documentary films. Ray is an excellent writer and it was he, more than anyone else, who showed me how to write and who gave me the opportunity and encouragement I needed during two tours at KPRC-TV, the NBC affiliate in Houston, where for many years he was news director.

Dan Rather of CBS News and Tom Jarriel of ABC News are two of the better known names touched by Ray Miller's life and example. There are scores of others.

I love and appreciate him almost as much as I did my own father and this book is my way of saying thanks to my teacher, my former boss, and my friend.

Enduring thanks also go to Tom Johnson, publisher of the *Los Angeles Times*, who "took a chance" on an unknown in 1984 and helped get me started as a nationally syndicated columnist.

To Willard Colston, Chairman of the Syndicate, and to its President, Lou Schwartz, and its Vice President for Sales, Doug

Mayberry, go special thanks for promoting me to editors around the country.

Thanks, too, to the Syndicate sales people who bombard editorial page editors in an attempt to get them to add me to their stable of columnists: Alan Shearer and Jim Lomenzo in New York, Fred Dingman in Chicago, and Gary Neelman in Salt Lake City.

And to those often-maligned copy editors who preserve me from libel suits by checking my facts, and from undeserved ridicule by checking my grammar: Don Michel, Steve Christensen, and Connie Cloos, who gets her name spelled correctly in THIS book, special thanks and warm appreciation.

INTRODUCTION

Occupied Territory

Conservatives, whether political or religious or both, have been struggling for several years to regain territory they surrendered without a fight. Their retreat from the intellectual and informational arena has created a vacuum that alternative world views have been unable to fill. The absence of a world view based on an enduring moral order has brought about the present social, economic, and political crises that now grip our land. In an information age, it is important that those who hold the key to the problems that beset us receive a hearing in the public arena.

For too long, conservatives have been content either to criticize the media or to publish and broadcast their views through their own outlets. That has had and will have little or no effect in promoting cultural change. Only a penetration of existing media structures and the proclamation of such views in the public arena will attract a large enough audience to make a difference.

I call this book *Occupied Territory* because it reflects my view that the editorial pages of the nation's newspapers are the territory, or marketplace of ideas, that must be penetrated and occupied in order to influence enough people to make a difference in our culture. I am "occupying" this territory, not in the militaristic sense, but as one who has managed to squeeze his way into a highly competitive field at a time when I believe the nation is ready to listen to the philosophy I represent.

The publisher of one of the nation's most influential newspapers said to me, "I believe you came along at just the right time. Look at the problems we confront: AIDS, the breakup of the family, alienation . . . everyone I know has run out of answers."

This awakening of the culture to the values and philosophy

1

held by conservatives provides an incredible opportunity, which if not seized will quickly be lost.

On a recent trip to Harvard, I visited the largest undergraduate class on campus. It has nothing to do with business or law. It is called "Jesus and the Moral Life." More than nine hundred students were enrolled in the class, about one-sixth of the total undergraduate enrollment at Harvard.

Professor Harvey Cox says he believes the renewed interest in religion and values by these and other Harvard students represents the first wave of a "post-Yuppie" generation's reaction against the materialism and self-directedness of the past twenty-five years. It is too early to say for sure, but if more than nine hundred students are carrying Bibles at Harvard, can revival be far behind?

Not every generation is privileged to help chart the course of history and strongly influence future generations. We have been given such a privilege, but with it comes a price. The price is relinquishing apathy and overcoming the fear of confrontation and opposition, and engaging the culture full force with the values and ideas that work.

In order to succeed at such a task, this engagement must take place in the arena where the other world view has held sway for the last generation. It does us no good to talk to ourselves, to "preach to the choir." We must compete where most people read and watch and listen. In an information age, this means the editorial pages of our nation's newspapers, television, radio, films, magazines; what has come collectively to be known as the "media."

The window of opportunity will not remain open forever. The nation has lost its compass and finds itself adrift in a sea of relativity, blown about by shifting winds of political and theological doctrine, and facing moral and political collapse. If positive change is to occur we must, as those at weddings with important information are requested to do, "speak now or forever hold our peace."

Our message should be, as the conservative philosopher Russell Kirk has noted, that there exists an enduring moral order. "That order," says Kirk, "is made for man, and man is made for it: human nature is constant, and moral truths are permanent."

Some dismiss such a notion by asking, "Whose morals and whose order shall be taught? After all, not everyone holds the same principles?" The obvious answer is, the moral order that has demonstrated consistency in its ability, in the words of the Preamble to the Constitution, "to provide for the common defense, promote the general welfare, and insure domestic tranquility."

Again, Russell Kirk has expressed it well: "This word order signifies harmony. There are two aspects or types of order: the inner order of the soul and the outer order of the commonwealth. Twenty-five centuries ago, Plato taught this doctrine, but even the educated nowadays find it difficult to understand. The problem of order has been a principle concern of conservatives ever since conservative became a term of politics.

"Our twentieth century world has experienced the hideous consequences of the collapse of belief in a moral order. Like the atrocities and disasters of Greece in the fifth century before Christ, the ruin of great nations in our century shows us the pit into which fall societies that mistake clever self-interest, or ingenious societal controls, for pleasing alternatives to an old-fangled moral order."

Is this not what has fueled the breakdown in the prevailing moral order? Whether it be scandals involving insider trading on Wall Street or the exercise of raw judicial power by judges who have ceased interpreting the law on the basis of certain self-evident truths and now are making the law based on their own philosophical self-interest, "looking out for number one" has replaced "in God we trust" as our national motto.

These columns, distributed by the Los Angeles Times Syndicate to more than fifty newspapers (at this writing), are an attempt by one journalist to reintroduce to our culture the importance of preserving a moral order. In book form they provide a permanent reference for those who wish to have such things. For those who live in cities where my column is not carried, I hope this book will serve as an impetus for you to contact the editorial page editor of your local paper and express an interest in having my columns published.

If you have not been reading your local paper, shame on you! Those who make decisions affecting your life read it, and in the absence of your opinions through letters to the editor and my opinions in my columns, how will such people know that you or I have something to say that is worthy of their consideration?

There is more than one price tag associated with attempting to occupy a portion of someone else's turf. It is the price of fierce opposition from those who pretend to believe in pluralism, freedom of expression, and open-mindedness. I deal with this in an epilogue. You will be amused and amazed at what you find there.

PART ONE

AN ENDURING
MORAL ORDER

WHATEVER BECAME OF SHAME?

We justify or excuse shameful behavior today, hiding behind the First Amendment. . . . So, because we stand for nothing, we fall for anything.

When the rock singer Madonna was asked about the nude photos of herself that appeared recently in the pages of *Playboy* and *Penthouse*, she commented: "I have never done anything I am ashamed of."

Some years ago, the noted psychiatrist, Dr. Karl Menninger, wrote a book called, *Whatever Became of Sin?* Perhaps someone ought to write one titled, *Whatever Became of Shame?*

The last time I recall hearing about shame as an emotion with which I should familiarize myself was when my grandmother corrected me for some long-forgotten act. "You should be ashamed of yourself," she said. As I recall, I was.

My mother once washed my mouth out with soap (a practice that has become culturally extinct), observing that I should be ashamed for something I had said. I do not recall using the word "shame" with my own children, but it is time for the word and the corrective behavior it can evoke to be exhumed.

Shame is defined as "a painful emotion cause by consciousness of guilt, shortcoming, or impropriety." This, of course, presupposes that one is familiar with the concept of guilt, a standard from which one may fall short and a sense of what is proper and what is not.

A second definition of shame is "a condition of humiliating disgrace or disrepute." There are few public figures these days who feel gripped by humiliation, disgrace, or disrepute when caught in what used to be considered shameful behavior.

When the late Congressman Adam Clayton Powell flaunted himself in public office (and in his not-so-private-life on the island of Bimini) twenty years ago, he explained that he was only following the example of some other members of Congress. No shame. No remorse.

The same sentiment was present in the Watergate affair. The conspirators wrote books, but none expressed shame for what they had done (with the exception of Charles Colson).

We justify or excuse shameful behavior today, hiding behind the First Amendment, or our reluctance to tell anyone what to do. We cringe at standard-setting for fear of being charged with forcing our moral view down the throats of others. So, because we stand for nothing, we fall for anything.

Even in the Vanessa Williams case, where the former Miss America wound up in *Penthouse*, there was no shame. Anger and litigation, yes, but not shame.

Those concerned about the rapid secularization of America can point to the scarcity of shame in the culture as proof that their concern is not unfounded. With the elimination of even minimal absolutes, there is a transvaluing of values whereby, as George Orwell clearly understood, evil becomes good.

Dr. Richard C. Halverson, the Senate chaplain, says he sees this absence of shame not just in public life, but in all of life. "It is another expression of the narcissism in our culture," he says. "If I do something and I like it, then it is right. I am my own judge and jury."

The thought finds its expression in something Judy Goldsmith, president of the National Organization for Women, said during a recent demonstration: "We will control our bodies and our lives." It is the ultimate expression of existentialism. The only thing that matters is what I am now doing for me. There is no other meaning to life.

Six years ago, *New Times* magazine had it right when it said in an editorial, "We shrug off almost everything now, moving on —with a lot of help from the omnivorous media—to the next fleeting titillation . . . Bianca Jagger, Billy Carter, Gary Gilmore —all hype, show, diversion. There's a new rock group called The Dead Kennedys. Shrug.

"It's as if we're beyond making distinctions, beyond caring."

What about Abscam? Some go to jail claiming innocence. One tells of having sex with his wife on the Capitol steps. The wife appears nude in *Playboy*. Nothing to be ashamed about. All the checks cleared.

Does anyone recall hearing a convicted criminal issuing a statement like this before heading for jail: "I was wrong. I am ashamed of myself. I ask your forgiveness. I deserve what I'm getting"? I don't.

So why should Madonna feel ashamed? Besides, what else can one expect from a "Material Girl"?

July 18, 1985

DRUGBALL

We are seeing in sports what we have seen occur in other institutions: the natural consequence of losing a "definable moral center" in the quest for personal rights and pleasure.

The descent of professional sports from the pedestal on which we once placed our idols began, I think, when Joe Namath slipped into a pair of pantyhose and reclined on our television screens. More recently, Jim Palmer has shown us his underwear, and who knows how many former athletes and umpires have touted the supposed virtues of light beer?

While growing up, we all knew that ballplayers wore underwear (though not pantyhose), and that they probably imbibed on occasion, if not regularly—but surely they were above cocaine and amphetamines.

During the tempest raised by revelations of drug use in professional sports, there has been a lot of talk about symptoms and not too much discussion about the cause. Howard Cosell got it right, though, when he was asked by David Hartman on "Good Morning America" why drugs have become such a problem in professional (and even some amateur) sports. Said Cosell, "There is no definable moral center in America anymore . . . and that is a problem for the entire culture."

Cosell, who is frequently given to overstatement on "Monday Night Football," is right on target with this observation. We are seeing in sports what we have seen occur in other institutions: the natural consequence of losing a "definable moral center" in the quest for personal rights and pleasure. This vacuum has brought us a period in which rights are paramount and responsibilities need not be discussed.

Watson Spoelstra, a retired Detroit sportswriter, tells me he is not surprised by the latest reports of drug use by professional ball players. "I saw this coming, maybe six years ago," he says. "I used to watch the Pittsburgh Pirates getting off the team bus in Atlanta. They'd pile out of that bus like a bunch of animals. It was obvious many were on something."

Darrell Porter, who now catches for the St. Louis Cardinals, came through his own personal hell while he was with the Kansas City Royals. Porter got hooked on alcohol first and then became dependent on even stronger drugs. Porter, who enrolled in a drug rehabilitation program, says, "Drugs are a lie and a cheat because they tell you there's a quick shortcut to happiness and fulfillment."

Porter wrote a book about his experiences called *Snap Me Perfect: The Darrell Porter Story*, in which he tells how the rehabilitation program helped him beat his drug problem and how a spiritual conversion gave him a new outlook on life.

Porter says ballplayers have too much idle time and too much money, and often turn to drugs as a means of escape.

He says, "The pressure to perform well and the general immaturity of young men thrust into success too soon along with the numerous temptations, especially on the road, have led many players down the wrong path."

There has been a lot said about the shame that the drug scandals have brought to the ball park and how it might affect public support for sports. But the shame felt by players, if any, should be no greater than the shame the junkies at Fourteenth and W Streets in Washington, D.C., ought to feel.

The *Washington Post* told the story of a street corner where unknown youths by the score have transformed a neighborhood into a twenty-four-hour-a-day, open-air heroin and cocaine market. These kids are no different from those who play the professional sports, except that no one outside the neighborhood knows their names and their faces are more likely to appear on a police mug shot than on a bubblegum card.

Most people will show no more concern for the drugged pro ball players (except in a curious way) than they will for the youths at Fourteenth and W in Washington. We don't have much time for caring anymore. As Andy Griffith observed about an injured player in his old comedy routine called "What It Was Was Football," "they'd just tote him off and run another on."

Athletes have become machines. When they become unproductive and we feel they have failed us, we are always ready to "tote them off and run another on." We rationalize that they are paid well and the players appear willing to uphold their end of the bargain by living well. That frees the rest of us from having to worry about "definable moral centers," and lets us get on with the business of pursuing happiness.

So, as Pete Rose hits one for the record books, and the playoffs beckon, we might consider a rewrite of the last line of baseball's most famous poem: "There is no joy in Mudville, mighty Casey is strung out."

September 19, 1985

THREE

THE POLITICS OF *AIDS*

Sex is not a constitutional right, like free speech, that can be exercised at will with no consequences.

Neuro fibromatosis. Epidermolysis bullosa. Tuberous sclerosis.

You are not reading typographical errors. These are three fatal diseases, all commonly referred to as Acquired Immune Deficiency Syndrome. They affect a very small number of Americans, but together they represent what now may be the world's most famous acronym: AIDS.

Not since the polio epidemic of the 1950s has so much public attention been heaped on a communicable disease as is currently the case with AIDS.

From the network newscasts to the front pages of newspapers to "Entertainment Tonight" (where one person said it is like breast cancer!) to "Larry King Live" (where a man claiming to be one of several of actor Rock Hudson's roommates expressed anger that somebody ratted on the actor and his disease), AIDS has replaced the African famine in the media's insatiable quest for something new.

Unlike polio before Salk and Sabin, AIDS is still largely preventable. The one thing the media does not want to say, because it fears being labeled "judgmental," is that the AIDS epidemic was launched by the promiscuous behavior of a subculture of homosexual and bisexual men who engaged in frequent and indiscriminate anal intercourse with other men. If they would stop that form of intercourse or at the very least take precautions, they would not get AIDS.

Dr. Alvin Friedman-Kine, an AIDS researcher at New York University, has said that AIDS will "probably prove to be the plague of the millennium." That is quite a strong statement considering the plagues this millennium has seen.

They include the bubonic plague, or Black Death, in fourteenth-century Europe. It killed ten thousand persons a day in Constantinople alone where it raged for four months. One-fourth of the population of Medieval Europe died.

The United States was hit by two cholera epidemics, one in 1830 and one in 1860. Dr. John Parascandola, chief medical historian at the National Institute of Health, says ten thousand people died within a few months in cities such as Cincinnati and St. Louis. In many cities and towns, one thousand deaths a month were not uncommon.

At the turn of the century tuberculosis was a major epidemic. And then there was polio in the 1950s.

In each of these epidemics, the national, state, or local governments did their best with what they had available in their day to end the scourges.

In fourteenth-century Europe, strict standards of cleanliness were imposed. Sick people, or those suspected of suffering from the plague, were isolated. Quarantines were imposed on imported food and visiting foreigners until their cleanliness could be assured.

During the nineteenth-century cholera epidemics, contaminated water sources were closed and quarantines were again implemented.

During the tuberculosis epidemic, sanitariums were established to separate the sick from the healthy. Cows found to be infected with the disease were confiscated and shot. Tainted milk was seized and destroyed.

In the polio epidemic of the 1950s, public pools were closed and people were urged to avoid crowded places. A massive educational campaign was conducted.

Now comes the AIDS epidemic, which has claimed 5,917 lives out of 11,871 reported cases. The Center for Disease Control in Atlanta says the number of AIDS cases will double in the next twelve months.

Most politicians fear the clout of homosexuals and are afraid to tell them to stop doing what causes the disease.

The public health authorities in San Francisco, after first trying to shut down the homosexual bath houses, which serve as breeding grounds for AIDS, caved in to pressure and are now distributing literature that tells homosexuals in detail how they can have "safe sex."

Do I lack compassion? Not at all. It is compassionate to tell people how to avoid contracting a dread disease even while looking for a cure for those who have it. The best way to avoid getting AIDS is not to engage in the activity that causes it.

With every freedom comes a measure of responsibility. The homosexuals started the AIDS epidemic (the bogus attempt to drag in Haitians notwithstanding), and it is now breaking out into the general population. The politicians and bureaucrats are hoping that a cure will be found before they are forced to take more drastic action. It is a race against time, for if AIDS reaches the state of a fourteenth-century Black Death, it may be extremely difficult to stop, and who knows how many innocent people might die? A cure could be a long way off, but prevention is available now.

Sex is not a constitutional right, like free speech, that can be exercised at will with no consequences. The *Journal of the American Medical Association* was correct when it said in a recent editorial that the best guarantee against getting AIDS is a monogamous, stable relationship. That attitude used to be called judgmental. Now it is called common sense.

August 1, 1985

FOUR

IN LIEU OF FLOWERS

These men were witnessing death and no amount of language manipulation could convince them otherwise.

Not long ago there was an unceremonial burial in Southern California. The public was not invited. No songs were sung. No poems were read. The immediate family was not in attendance, because they steadfastly refused to acknowledge that the dead ever existed. It was probably a unique event, because it involved the burial of nearly 16,500 (a) babies, (b) fetuses, (c) products of conception (take your choice), discovered in a shipping container in February, 1982; a discovery that set off what may have been the most intense court battle that has yet taken place over the abortion issue.

After months of litigation, the matter was brought to an end when the U.S. Supreme Court upheld the California Supreme Court's ruling that the fetuses must be disposed of without a religious ceremony planned by the Catholic League of Southern California. Peculiar, isn't it? The worth of the unborn depends upon the value assigned them by their mothers-to-be (or in these cases, "mothers-to-was"). They have no intrinsic worth. Yet, the American Civil Liberties Union and the Feminist Women's Health Center were supported by the courts in their argument that to allow prolife people with religious feelings to say some words over what they regard as dead babies would be to assign a value to the fetuses that is constitutionally prohibited. Some constitutional rights are apparently deserving of more protection than others.

The case dragged on for so long that many no doubt lost track of how it started or forgot the shock felt by those who first discovered the dead (and here I will use the non-Orwellian word) babies.

Fortunately, a young investigative reporter, S. Rickly Christian, has chronicled the story in a book called, *The Woodland Hills Tragedy* (Crossway Books). Christian and a young woman colleague retrace the events that led to the discovery of a large container in which the dead babies had been stored for disposal. Strangely, all 16,500 of them had at one time been buried in backyard containers belonging to Malvin R. Weisberg, who for nine years operated the "laboratory" to which the babies were sent following the abortions at various clinics and hospitals.

The most compelling part of the book comes when Christian and his colleague interview the men who transported the heavy container to a storage yard and accidentally discovered what was inside when the contents spilled on the ground.

Ron Gillette described his first reaction upon seeing the dead babies.

". . . it's filled with bodies . . . dismembered bodies."

Gillette's description of what he saw is that of an untrained, unsophisticated observer, which makes it all the more credible.

He speaks of seeing "hands, torn right off," of "grown men weeping and vomiting," not at the smell, but at the grim reality that what they were seeing could not be dismissed with euphemisms. These men were witnessing death and no amount of language manipulation could convince them otherwise.

Later, when reporters arrive, Gillette says he felt like telling them, "YOU stand there and stare at a ripped-apart baby for fifteen minutes like I did. YOU stand there and count the fingers and look at legs with little kneecaps that have been tore off the body. YOU stand there and try to find the head, only to realize there ain't no head. YOU do that just like I did. And then you tell me how YOU feel."

An interesting challenge to the press and to the public.

More than just a rehash of an old news story, *The Woodland Hills Tragedy* is a superb insight into the abortion industry itself. One paragraph, in particular, exposes the greed that is the driving force behind much of the rapid growth in the business of abortion.

"We enter the hospital parking lot from the back alley, and suddenly it's as if we're on Rodeo Drive in Beverly Hills. The reserved spaces are occupied by glistening luxury cars. A white Cadillac and several late-model foreign cars line the back wall of the hospital. I pull into a space beside a silver Mercedes Turbo-diesel 300 SD. . . ."

It is hard to explain away reality to a person who has seen it. That is why anti-Semites cannot convince us that the Holocaust is fiction. We've seen the pictures. We've heard from the survivors and even some of the perpetrators.

It is the same with the abortion tragedy, now approaching the twenty-five million mark.

In the words of the uneducated and unsophisticated Ron Gillette, who saw what he saw and knows that what he felt was real and who doesn't need a lawyer or a sociologist or an "expert" to tell him he was hallucinating, "I believe each of them babies was coming into this world with a job to do. This generation, our generation, can only go so far. Then the next one has to take over. That's the way I learned it. But a big part of the next generation is mangled up and thrown away like garbage. Discarded like them babies in the container."

Don't worry, Ron. If people read this book and see the pictures of what you saw with your own eyes, perhaps they will stop this killing, and if they do, then the lives of those babies will have served a very worthwhile purpose.

September 12, 1985

FIVE

THIS ARTICLE IS RATED "R"

. . . How could [Ben Franklin] be expected to know anything about church-state separation . . . ? He only helped to write the Constitution.

The following article is rated "R," which means it contains material not suitable for anyone under seventeen, unless accompanied by a parent or guardian, or unless the child attends a Baltimore public school.

The Baltimore city schools want to conduct a "sex survey" for students in the seventh through twelfth grades. The test is necessary, say school officials, because there were ninety-seven live births to girls between ten and fourteen last year and more than three thousand births to all girls in the Baltimore school system. Baltimore enjoys the dubious distinction of having one of the highest teen pregnancy rates in the country, despite its incorporation of Planned Parenthood-based sex education courses since 1967.

And so, what is the school system's response to its problem? Why, more sex education, of course. It is the moral equivalent of asking chemical companies to clean up the rivers by dumping more pollutants into them.

Though the sex survey has been twice "deferred" due to public outcries, and seventh graders are no longer involved, again because of protests from parents, the questions are enough to make a ninth or eleventh grader squirm and drive their parents into the arms of tuition tax credits and private schools.

Some examples: "What do you think is the best age for a female to have sex for the first time? For a male?"

"How good do you think each of these ways are of keeping a

female from getting pregnant?" (The surveyors could use some help with their grammar, which is obviously not as important as these questions): "(a) sponge, (b) diaphragm (c) condom (rubbers) (d) IUD (loop coil) (e) rhythm (safe time of month) (f) cream, jelly, foam, or suppositories (g) pill (h) withdrawal (pulling out) (i) douche (washing out the vagina)."

How about this question: "I think it's all right to have an abortion (choose as many as you want): (a) if the female has been raped (b) if the female is under fifteen (c) if the pregnancy is a risk to the female's health (d) if the unborn baby is known to be defective (e) if the female doesn't want a baby for any reason (f) never."

The questionnaire also wants to know whether the students have ever had "wet dreams" and "whether you have ever 'come' from masturbating," and, if yes, how old they were the first time. It asks whether the children have ever had sex, how old they were the first time, how many times they have had sex in the last four weeks, the most times in a month, and whether the boys have ever gotten a girl pregnant. It also asks if they are religious and whether they have been to religious services in the last four weeks.

Education "experts" in Baltimore say that these questions must be asked so that a proper curriculum can be developed to reduce unwanted pregnancies and other consequences of sex outside of marriage.

But a curriculum has already been developed. It was first published by the National Education Association (NEA) in 1941 in *The American Citizens Handbook*. Once you've read it, you will not be surprised that the NEA would like to have each copy back.

The NEA handbook quotes with obvious approval Ben Franklin's plan to produce a good citizen. Under the heading, "The Virtues and Their Precepts," Franklin included chastity. Yes, CHASTITY, which he defined as "clean thoughts and wholesome activities (that) lead to clean living." Franklin also advised under "humility" to imitate Jesus and Socrates, but then how could he be expected to know anything about church-state separation in the 1980s? He only helped to write the Constitution.

Later in the NEA handbook, Horace Mann, one of the founders of American public school education, is quoted from a speech he delivered in Boston on July 4, 1842: "In every course of studies, all the practical and perceptive parts of the Gospel should have been sacredly included." Would this include what Franklin referred to as chastity? Surely Mann thought so.

Mann also said that people who neglect the education of their children in these matters will get licentiousness instead of liberty; violence and chicanery instead of law; superstition and craft instead of religion; and the self-indulgence of all sensual and unhallowed passions instead of happiness. Mann must have had a telescopic view of the Baltimore public schools in 1986.

Imagine future generations studying the history of education in America. They first read the inspiring words of Ben Franklin and Horace Mann, and then they read the sex survey from the Baltimore public school system inquiring about the number of "wet dreams" students have experienced.

This is going to reduce unwanted pregnancies? This is merely going to give the kids the green light to go further.

One can rejoice that the survey has been "deferred" at least for now. One must despair that it probably will be taken, not only in Baltimore but in other American public schools unless parents make their wishes known, and fast.

January 12, 1986

SIX

TAKING THE HYPOCRITICAL OATH

*If you are reading this . . . you have survived abortion and infanti-
cide, but you are just one accident away from admission to the twilight
zone of brain damage that could lead doctors to finish what the accident
failed to do.*

At its annual convention in New Orleans, the American
Medical Association took another one of those small steps for
medicine that frequently produces giant leaps backward for
mankind.

The AMA announced a change in its policy on when to "pull
the plug" on patients in "irreversible" comas. The new opinion
says a doctor's social commitment is to "sustain life." The old
opinion said it was to "prolong life."

It may seem like semantical hair-splitting, but the distinction
is an important one in a nation where it is legal to abort unwanted babies until the moment of live birth, and to deprive of
life a newly born handicapped baby when doctors clairvoyantly
determine that the child cannot have a "meaningful life." Under
such circumstances, the significance of the AMA policy change
should not be taken lightly.

Put it this way: if you are reading this, you have survived
abortion and infanticide, but you are just one accident away
from admission to the twilight zone of brain damage that could
lead doctors to finish what the accident failed to do.

U.S. Surgeon General Dr. C. Everett Koop tells me, "The
major issue before this country is whether we are willing to consider a bed, a blanket, and fluids as rights, or only as treatment,
like antibiotics. All of our future hinges on this debate."

Koop says that Baby Doe cases involving handicapped infants "have hoisted us on our own petard. Congress has made it clear that the handicapped child may not be deprived of treatment and now [the AMA] says that the elderly or comatose may be deprived of such treatment. It is impossible to have it both ways."

Robert Barry, a highly educated priest (three master's degrees and a Ph.D.), is studying, under a National Endowment for the Humanities Fellowship, the thoughts of Catholic ethicists on giving food and water to the nonterminally ill (including the comatose, handicapped, elderly, and other medically vulnerable persons). Father Barry charges that "the AMA has declared war" on such people.

Father Barry says that the AMA has moved beyond the categories neurologists formerly made between a brain-damaged person (one who is aware of what is taking place around him) and a comatose person (one who is usually not aware). Now it believes doctors should be able to deprive the less severely ill of food and fluids they need to stay alive when a doctor determines, often arbitrarily, that a person is no longer fit to live.

It does seem to be the ultimate answer to the question of what to do with damaged merchandise. Now we can contemplate throwing a human being away as we do a car we have totaled or a soft drink can after the contents have been drained.

For those who take the time to read what the eugenicists are saying, the AMA's subtle shift should come as no surprise.

Australian "ethicist" Peter Singer, writing in the July, 1983, issue of *Pediatrics*, said, "We can no longer base our ethics on the idea that human beings are a special form of creation, made in the image of God, singled out from all other animals, and alone possessing an immortal soul."

Having removed the protective layer of man's uniqueness, Singer then expressed precisely what the AMA has expressed by changing its ethical standards: "If we compare a severely defective human infant with a nonhuman animal, a dog or a pig, for example, we will often find the nonhuman to have superior capacities, both actual and potential, for rationality, self-consciousness, communication, and anything else that can be plausibly considered morally significant."

The Nazis tried eugenics. They were unsuccessful, but it

took a world war to stop them. The American medical community, ably assisted by technology and some of those ever-present
clergy who can always be relied on to give their blessing to
almost any horror, are proceeding down the eugenics slope with
virtually no opposition.

Unless you can guarantee that you will never be critically ill
or injured and that you will die in your own bed at a ripe old
age, you had better be concerned about this.

March 23, 1986

SOME VICTIMS ARE MORE EQUAL THAN OTHERS

AIDS stopped being a "civil rights" issue when homosexuals and some heterosexuals began dying.

If a forward journey of one thousand miles is to be taken in increments of single steps, so too must a journey that leads one on a retreat.

The latest step in retreat in the continuing controversy over the disease AIDS, and the mostly homosexual male population that suffers from it, involves the insurance industry.

In what is thought to be the first incident of its kind in the nation, the city council of Washington, D.C., has approved a bill that prohibits health and life insurance companies from denying coverage to persons who test positively for the AIDS virus. The bill does not cover those who have contracted AIDS; only those who are shown to be carrying the AIDS virus.

The problem with the "reasoning" is that as many as 5 percent of those who are now tested and found to be carrying the AIDS virus will develop the disease, according to a National Cancer Institute study published in the February 28, 1986, *Science Magazine*. And every new piece of information that is discovered about AIDS tends to push the percentage higher.

According to the August, 1985, issue of *Annals of Internal Medicine*, a Danish study has found that 90 percent of male homosexuals with AIDS antibodies eventually show some damage to their immune system.

So, what we have in the District of Columbia is a political

and not a scientific or medical decision. It is the latest in a series of attempts to confer legitimacy on the homosexual lifestyle. But now that effort by politicians is flying in the face of a growing body of evidence that homosexual practice can be hazardous to the health not only of homosexuals but of the wider population as well.

Rob Bier, spokesman for the Insurance Association of America, was among those lobbying the hardest against the bill. Bier says non-homosexual persons are being discriminated against because they will be forced to subsidize insurance for a special class of people who must now be judged by standards that differ from those by which everyone else must live.

Bier says that an insurance industry formula generally denies coverage to persons who are in a risk category that is between four and five times greater than that of a person in reasonably good health. With AIDS, he says, those who have the antibodies in their blood are at twenty times the risk of the average person.

Bier says he was pleasantly surprised when both Ralph Nader's National Insurance Consumer's Organization and the American Civil Liberties Union supported the insurance industry's position against granting an exemption to the carriers of the AIDS virus when no such exemption is offered to persons with any other malady.

Bier, who tells me he is a diabetic, says he is thinking seriously of joining the local diabetic association and petitioning the city council to grant him special protection. He says he cannot get insurance because of his diabetes and must receive whatever life and health benefits he can from his wife's policy. He says if homosexuals are to receive special treatment, he should, too.

AIDS stopped being a "civil rights" issue when homosexuals and some heterosexuals began dying. No one has a right to unleash such a disease on a people and then hide behind the all-purpose defense of "discrimination."

Politicians, especially those on the D.C. city council, obviously fear defeat more than they do the response of a community that is bound to rebel should AIDS ever get out of control. But the council members, as well as those elected to even higher office at the state and national levels, must be held accountable as they continue to march us backwards, away from a sound and logical policy in the handling of insurance, and away from a policy to deal with the most serious disease to strike humanity since the bubonic plague of the Middle Ages.

May 22, 1986

EIGHT

THE TIME IS NOW

If Ronald Reagan sincerely believes that God spared his life for a purpose, does he believe that purpose was solely to give Americans lower mortgage interest rates and reduced gasoline prices while abortion on demand continues unabated?

Early in 1984, during an interview with three Washington Post reporters, President Reagan was asked what would be his "central purpose" and "what would you want most to accomplish" in a second term.

After running through the economic goals, most of which will have been achieved when tax reform is fully implemented, the President cited as a central purpose of a second term "treatment of the problem of abortion."

In virtually every other category mentioned by the President as a central concern, there has been action. Only abortion remains the outstanding issue on which the President has said, "I am going to fight as long and hard as I can." Unfortunately, he has fought neither long nor hard.

It is not for a lack of rhetoric that abortions have not been stopped. The President's statements on the subject would fill a small book. He has said, "I happen to believe that in an abortion we are taking a human life." And he has called abortion a "moral sin that is violating our very constitutional guarantee of right to life."

In fact, a few years ago, the President did fill a small book with his thoughts on abortion. It was called *Abortion and the Conscience of a Nation*. In it he argues, "The real question today is not when human life begins, but WHAT IS THE VALUE OF HUMAN LIFE" [emphasis his]. He also said, "My administration is dedicated to the preservation of America as a free land,

and THERE IS NO CAUSE MORE IMPORTANT FOR PRESERVING THAT FREEDOM [emphasis mine] than affirming the transcendent right to life of all human beings, the right without which no other rights have any meaning."

No one questions the President's sincerity in wishing to stop abortion. No doubt we can expect new initiatives coming from the White House that might include a push for a permanent Hyde Amendment, forever barring federal funds for abortions and denying such funds to any organization that performs them. Mr. Reagan has said as much in his recent messages to Congress. But such a strategy will do little more than slow the rate of abortion, which has now snuffed out nearly nineteen million lives since 1973.

What is needed is an effort similar to that employed for the President's economic agenda. This effort should not focus initially on a problematic legislative solution, but instead it should concentrate on forging a strong majority consensus that allowing abortion on demand was a mistake and must be reversed. Unless large numbers of Americans are clamoring for change, neither Congress nor the courts will do much.

The President will never get from Congress what he is unwilling to provide on his own. On economic and defense matters he has gone directly to the people via television and public speeches to convince them of the correctness of his position.

Now that the economy is back in shape and America's military capability and resolve have been restored, it is only an activist President who can stop the killing.

In a letter last January to White House Chief of Staff Donald Regan, five members of Congress (Representatives Chris Smith, Henry Hyde, Jack Kemp, Vin Weber, and Senator Gordon Humphrey) said, "We believe that a presidential address could serve as a major catalyst in the stepped-up effort to reverse Roe vs. Wade. The address itself is likely to save thousands of lives due to a heightened awareness about the child's life. We believe the President could help educate and sensitize the nation practically overnight and thus accelerate the day when the unborn children enjoy legal protection."

The day after he was shot, the President was visited by the

now late Terence Cardinal Cooke. The President told Cardinal Cooke, "Whatever days are left to me are His."

If Ronald Reagan sincerely believes that God spared his life for a purpose, does he believe that purpose was solely to give Americans lower mortgage interest rates and reduced gasoline prices while abortion on demand continues unabated?

Do Americans honor their Presidents because of their fiscal policies? The National Park Service says there is not a single monument or memorial to a President for his economic accomplishments.

During the 1980 campaign, the slogan of the Republican ticket was, "The Time is Now for Reagan." The time is now to stop abortion.

If President Reagan will not mount such a campaign, he is not likely to have any permanent, visible monument to his Presidency, and whatever else he may have accomplished will pale in comparison to what might have been achieved.

May 18, 1986

GAY RIGHTS,
GAY WRONGS

The Justices read the New York Times.

In some ways the Supreme Court's five-four decision upholding Georgia's sodomy law defies analysis.

As Oscar Hammerstein wrote, "Who can explain it? Who
can tell you why? Fools give you reasons. Wise men never try."

Who can explain a Supreme Court that in one case finds a
constitutional right to privacy that allows a woman to abort the
product of a heterosexual act between herself and a man, yet
finds no such right to privacy between members of the same sex
performing acts of sodomy that do not result in such a product?
It defies logic, but it is indicative of what happens when a court
and a culture have lost their compass.

Constitutional attorney John Whitehead, president of the
Rutherford Institute, believes that "without the spread of AIDS,
this opinion would not have come down the way it did."

Whitehead sees the decision as another example of sociological
jurisprudence. "The Justices read the *New York Times*," he says.

Realizing this was a critical case for their continued drive to
gain legitimacy, the homosexual position was argued in the
Georgia court by Harvard's Laurence Tribe. Tribe contended
that the basic issue in the case was whether his client, Michael
Hardwick, could be told by the state of Georgia how to behave
sexually in the privacy of his own home with another consenting
male adult. Hardwick had been arrested and charged by Atlanta
police while committing sodomy with a consenting man in the
bedroom of his home.

Assistant Attorney General for Georgia Michael Hobbs

countered that nothing in the Constitution guarantees a right to engage in homosexual acts and that the document must not become an "instrument for changing social order." But it is precisely because the Constitution HAS been used as an instrument for changing social order that we have cases like these.

A preview of this decision was handed down by Judge Robert Bork of the D.C. Circuit Court of Appeals in 1984. Said Judge Bork, "We would find it impossible to conclude that a right to homosexual conduct is fundamental or implicit in the concept of ordered liberty, unless any and all private sexual behavior falls within those categories, a conclusion we're unwilling to draw."

Even more to the point in rejecting an absolute right to privacy was a dissenting opinion in a 1980 New York Court of Appeals case, The People vs. Onofre, which said, ". . . if the only criterion for determining when particular conduct should be deemed to be constitutionally protected is whether the conduct affects society in a direct and tangible way, then it is difficult to perceive how a state may lawfully interfere with such consensual practices as euthanasia, marijuana smoking, prostitution, and homosexual marriage."

There is an even greater message in the court's ruling on the Georgia sodomy statute. It is the importance of the elevation of Justice William Rehnquist to Chief Justice. Rehnquist has been the court's strongest state's rights advocate. It may be safely predicted that more state's rights cases will now be decided in favor of the states. And, as Justice Lewis Powell was the key vote on this case, one might expect to see Powell succumbing more regularly to the new Chief Justice's rightward gravitational pull.

The narrow verdict in the Georgia sodomy case gives no reason for conservatives to rejoice that the Justices have "seen the light" and have undergone a kind of spiritual conversion. What the court has seen is the darkness proceeding out of the rapidly increasing number of AIDS cases. It knows, the media disinformation campaign notwithstanding, that AIDS began primarily because of anal intercourse between males and then moved out to infect people by other means. It also knows that public health experts are predicting that AIDS could become the worst plague in human history unless something is done to stop its spread.

In the Georgia case the court saw a chance to set a legal limit to such behavior, or at least a limit of legal tolerance. It seized, however narrowly, on that chance.

Had the court legitimized sodomy throughout the country by striking down the Georgia statute, it would have sent the wrong signal at a time when caution and even celibacy among homosexuals ought to be what is called for.

This is a time to focus, not on "gay pride," or on "gay rights," but on "gay wrongs."

July 6, 1986

WHAT'S AN ORGY?

If chastity until marriage were ever to become a national trend again, Planned Parenthood might be in danger of losing a good portion of its federal subsidy.

Imagine for a moment this scene. Your child comes home from school, throws her books on the table and instead of asking "What's for dinner?" wants to know "What's an orgy?"

This is a scene that Planned Parenthood of Maryland wants to see repeated all over the city of Baltimore in one of the goofiest ideas ever to be forced on the public. A Planned Parenthood of Maryland spokesman says the ad campaign is designed to get children and their parents talking about sex. The ad contains a warning to parents: "If your kids aren't asking you (what an orgy is), they may be asking for trouble."

There can be no question that Baltimore has a problem. Baltimore has the highest teen pregnancy rate for a city of its size in the nation. Twenty-five percent of all births there are to teens. But is "What's an orgy?" likely to reduce teen pregnancies? No more than asking "What's a cigarette?" is likely to reduce smoking, or "What's a holdup?" will cut down on bank robberies.

Most information given teenagers about sex is unbalanced. Their music, magazines, films, and television tell them that sex is great, that it feels good and that everybody is doing it. But little is said through the information and entertainment systems young people rely on about the consequences of too-soon and irresponsible sex.

Why is it assumed by Planned Parenthood and the other so-called "sex experts" that young people won't respond to a positive approach to responsible sexual behavior? Instead they assume a defeatist attitude, one that says young people are going to be sexually active anyway, so let's keep them from getting pregnant and from acquiring a venereal disease.

Why can't a healthy discussion about sex between parent and child evolve from an ad campaign that features the question "What is chastity?", or "What is self-control?"

The answer, of course, is that Planned Parenthood has a vested interest in the sexual practices of the young. If chastity until marriage were ever to become a national trend again, Planned Parenthood would be in danger of losing a good portion of its federal subsidy. The "What's an orgy?" campaign has a better chance of producing more orgies than it does responsible sexual behavior. One is reminded of an old Pete Seeger song about the Vietnam War. Seeger wrote, "We're knee-deep in the big muddy, and the big fool says to push on."

We're knee-deep in the big muddy of teen pregnancies and the big fools are telling us to push on with more of the same: more valueless sex education, more free contraceptives without parental knowledge or consent, more abortion "services." This program has not worked—as Baltimore demonstrates—and it will not work.

Another Baltimore Institution, Johns Hopkins University, developed the "say no to premarital sex" program that resulted in a hit record by Tatiana and Johnny that is playing throughout Mexico. The Agency for International Development has provided $300,000 for the project.

If saying no to premarital sex is a good program for Mexico, why can't it be good for Baltimore and the rest of the country?

August 31, 1986

ELEVEN

THE TIDE IS TURNING

. . . A majority of women who have had abortions felt "forced" by outside circumstances into the procedure.

DENVER—One might have expected to find a pall hanging over the National Right to Life Convention following two defeats in a week at the hands of the Supreme Court. But in place of gloom, there was optimism that the thirteen-year-old abortion high tide is about to go out.

Down the street at the National Organization for Women Convention there were brave words that the "pro-choice" cause is supported by more Americans than ever before, but in her rational moments, NOW President Eleanor Smeal acknowledges that with the change of a single Supreme Court vote, the battle to keep abortion legal could be lost.

There is good reason for optimism by pro-life forces and it is only in part due to the numbers game. Pro-lifers should also be encouraged by the court's desperate attempts to cover its legal behind, as it increasingly resorts to tangled logic in order to preserve its "tradition" of not having to admit that it made a mistake. The court's desperation was on display when it struck down a Pennsylvania law requiring that a woman be given certain information about the abortion procedure, information roughly equivalent to what she is entitled by federal law to receive when she applies for a bank loan or considers her choices among competing brands of packaged, bottled, or canned goods at the supermarket.

Perhaps the greatest momentum the pro-life movement has going for it is a power source whose potential remains largely untapped: the enormous number of women who have had abortions and who now regret their decisions. Such women were more visible than ever at the National Right to Life Convention. There are indications from recent studies that these women, who describe themselves as "victims of" or "exploited by" abortion, are about to "roar in numbers too big to ignore."

In a national survey for a forthcoming book, *Women Exploited, A Nation Deceived*, author David C. Reardon found that a majority of women (63 percent) who have had abortions felt "forced" by outside circumstances into the procedure. Eighty-five percent said they would have kept their child "under better circumstances."

Those who said they felt "forced" to have abortions blamed their reluctant decisions on husbands, boyfriends, parents, doctors, or social workers. No more than one-third of the women interviewed said they felt free to make their own choice.

When approaching the abortion clinic, 45-61 percent said they were still hoping for another option. Over 91 percent felt that their counselors and doctors failed to help them explore their decisions.

The survey also refutes the "pro-choice" argument that "people are going to have abortions whether they are legal or not." Only 5-9 percent said they would have considered an abortion had it not been legally available. Over 75 percent stated they definitely would not have considered an abortion if it had not been legal.

Another survey, conducted by Anne Catherine Speckhard, Ph.D., University of Minnesota, found that many women suffer severe emotional and psychological stress for years following an abortion. This stress includes, according to the survey, hallucinations, perceived visitation from the aborted child, nightmares, feelings of "craziness," flashbacks of the abortion experience, and preoccupation with the aborted child.

More than 70 percent of the women interviewed experienced one or more of these reactions following their abortions: discomfort with children, decreased ability to experience emotions, a feeling they had been victimized, low self-worth, preoccupation with aborted child, fear that others will learn of the abortion, feelings of guilt, anger, and depression and, in 100 percent of the cases, feelings of grief, sadness, regret, and loss.

Some describe these women who have had abortions as a

"time bomb," because their problems only begin to manifest themselves five to seven years after the abortion.

With more than ten million women having had abortions since 1973, this time bomb may be about to go off with a force that could shatter even the Supreme Court.

June 19, 1986

TWELVE

DOCTORS WHO KILL

Nazi doctors destroyed the boundary between healing and killing.

In a new book, *The Nazi Doctors: Medical Killing and the Psychology of Genocide*, author Robert Jay Lifton reminds us that even physicians, whom we tend to trust more than other professionals, need to be watched, lest they become willing participants in plans by the state to rob certain classes of citizens of their endowed and inalienable right to life.

Lifton details how Nazi doctors destroyed the boundary between healing and killing. These deathcamp doctors, notes Lifton, did not see themselves as mass murderers but as part of the program not only to make a better Germany but also to perform a service to their "patients," none of whose lives, they believed, were worth living.

The parallels between the first steps of the Nazi program and one recently instituted by the state of California are close enough to be chilling.

"The Nazis justified direct medical killing," writes Lifton, "by use of the simple concept of 'life unworthy of life.'" This program began with coercive sterilizations and was followed by the killing of "impaired" children in hospitals, then the killing of "impaired" adults, then the mass extermination of those regarded as the most "impaired" of all: the Jews.

It was a step-by-step approach, carried out in utmost secrecy. The philosophical foundation based on the Hegelian view of "rational utility," leading to the replacement of moral, ethical, and religious values, was established even before Hitler came to power. The groundwork laid, physicians began killing only the most "extreme" cases. Once the door had been opened, it became easier to kill the less "extreme" cases until all distinctions disappeared.

The California program requires every physician in the state to offer a genetic screening test to every pregnant patient. If the patient refuses the offer (which could sound like a recommendation), she must sign a statement which says she is willing to accept the consequences. The pressure is clearly on the patient to allow the test.

Dr. Philip B. Dreisbach, a member of the American Board of Internal Medicine and Medical Oncology, calls this a "eugenics program which fits the mold of Planned Parenthood founder Margaret Sanger's philosophy to 'create a race of thoroughbreds.'" The names, addresses, and phone numbers of the patients identified as carrying handicapped infants are turned over to genetic counselors who will then presumably advise the mothers on the wisdom of permanent birth control or sterilization, not to mention aborting the baby they are carrying, whatever the potential handicap, even though many of these handicaps, such as spina bifida, can often be repaired after birth.

The program, like that of the Third Reich, centralizes information under the authority of a single government entity. In this case, it is the California Department of Health.

In 1946 and 1947, Leo Alexander, a Boston psychiatrist, was consultant to the U.S. Secretary of War and served with the office of Chief of Counsel for War Crimes in Nuremberg. In a paper, Alexander outlined the problem: "[The Holocaust] started with the acceptance of the attitude that there is such a thing as a life not worthy to be lived."

We must not be blind to the connection between the doctors of forty years ago who destroyed the boundary between healing and killing and those of today who, innocently or knowingly, have done the same.

September 25, 1986

THIRTEEN

GETTING SERIOUS ABOUT TOBACCO

At a time when scientists search for the causes of diseases for which there are no known cures, one would think there might be greater support for eliminating a scourge that does not have to exist.

The federal government has issued a ban on smoking except in designated areas in all 7,500 federal buildings. The nearly total prohibition on smoking in the federal workplace, effective February 8, has been a long time coming, and ought to be extended by Congress to every enclosed public area. Non-smokers should be freed from inhaling the acrid smoke of nicotine addicts, who may have the right to kill themselves and smell bad, but who have no right to do it unto others.

Other than a dead skunk, there is nothing that smells worse or offends more than a cigarette smoker puffing (and usually coughing) away, oblivious to what he or she is doing to the air and the people nearby.

Recently the government became serious about its anti-drug campaign. Unfortunately, it left nicotine off its list of hazardous substances, even though nicotine is a drug that has hooked about 30 percent of the country. More people are addicted to cigarettes than to cocaine.

Smoking is said to be linked to the death of 350,000 Americans annually and, according to the World Health Organization, more than one million people die each year from tobacco-associated diseases worldwide. Cigarettes are the No. 1 cause of preventable death in America today. At a time when scientists search for the causes of diseases for which there are no known cures, one would think there might be greater support for eliminating a scourge that does not have to exist.

The news about tobacco keeps getting worse. It was reported last week by the University of Southern California School of Medicine that cigarette smoking has been linked to cancer of the pancreas. The National Academy of Sciences said last month that exposure to smoking in the home appears to double the chance of respiratory disease in children.

And yet, with all we know about the hazards of tobacco, there is no national clamor for greater restrictions on cigarette smoking and the banning of advertising that encourages people to indulge in the practice.

In an excellent article in the December issue of *The Quill*, a magazine for journalists, Dr. Alan Blume, a New York physician and founder of Doctors Ought to Care (DOC), charges that the press is guilty of a conflict of interest because it receives millions of dollars in advertising from the tobacco industry and goes easy on that industry in its reporting.

"Tobacco," notes Dr. Blum, "is the world's most heavily advertised and promoted product. In the United States, tobacco use is backed by advertising budgets of more than $2 billion."

Even though tobacco advertising accounts for only about 1 percent of all U.S. newspaper ad revenue, the industry is reluctant to part with it.

But Harris Rayl, editor and publisher of the *Salina Journal* in Salina, Kansas, writes in *The Quill* that his paper has won back much more in respect from readers than it has lost in advertising revenue by refusing to publish tobacco advertisements.

Arguments over First Amendment rights and whether newspapers ought to play the role of your mother are "a diversion," says Rayl. "Most newspapers are unwilling to give up tobacco advertising for one reason: money. . . . We still run news stories about the tobacco industry and its products, and we leave in all the self-serving quotes from the tobacco people. We accept letters to the editor from the tobacco companies as well. But we think splashy full-page advertisements hawking cigarettes as tickets to maturity and glamour go too far."

So do I. If the federal government regards smoking as a serious enough health threat to ban the practice in all but designated areas of its buildings, those of us in journalism ought to bite the bullet (or in this case, the filter) and refrain from promoting a substance the use of which has prompted the following warnings form the Surgeon General: "Smoking causes lung cancer, heart disease, emphysema, and may complicate pregnancy; smoking by pregnant women may result in fetal injury, premature birth, and low birth weight; quitting smoking now greatly reduces serious risks to your health; the Surgeon General has determined that cigarette smoking is dangerous to health."

December 14, 1986

FOURTEEN

COME BACK IN TWENTY-FOUR HOURS

The once tightly-rolled ideological string ball of the pro-abortion forces is beginning to unravel.

The decision by the Supreme Court to consider whether states may require minors to notify their parents of their decision to seek an abortion and then to wait twenty-four hours before obtaining one, may be considered a victory by those who oppose abortion. In fact it obscures the overriding issue.

The core of the argument over abortion is, as the Court noted in a 1973 ruling, whether the fetus is a "person" within the parameters of the Constitution. If it is, then all abortions ought to be illegal. If fetuses are not persons, then no law, including one that mandates a twenty-four-hour waiting period, makes much sense.

All the same, the once tightly-rolled ideological string ball of the pro-abortion forces is beginning to unravel. Three recent incidents make that point.

The first involves twenty-seven-year-old Pamela Rae Stewart Monson of El Cajon, California. Monson faces criminal charges in the death of her infant son because she allegedly failed to summon medical help when she began hemorrhaging the day her son was born. The child was born with massive brain damage allegedly caused by Monson's use of amphetamines and marijuana during her pregnancy. The baby died six weeks later.

Had it been revealed in a test during Monson's pregnancy that her son was brain damaged and had she, at that time, decided to have an abortion, she would not be facing criminal prosecution for "fetal neglect." Only the light of day, this suggests, imparts to babies the Constitutional rights enjoyed by the rest of us.

Columnist Ellen Goodman has wondered in print whether this case proves that society's focus on the rights of the fetus has gone too far. That is an interesting question since pro-choicers like Goodman used to focus *all* their attention on the unborn baby, saying it was not human life, or not a person, or too small to survive outside the womb until relatively close to the time of delivery. Now that science, with increasingly more miraculous procedures, is saving babies at earlier stages of development pro-choicers want to change the rules.

This brings me to the second case.

Doctors in San Francisco during a pioneering procedure recently removed a twenty-three week old fetus from his mother's womb. Surgeons successfully cleared a blocked urinary tract and returned the fetus to its mother's uterus. The pronoun "his" and the noun "baby" were used by the *New York Times* to describe the entity receiving the doctors' attention.

Question: Since the Supreme Court has said that no one is a person until he/she is delivered from the womb, was this thing that was operated upon not a person before the surgery, but acquired personhood during the surgical procedure (because he was outside the mother's body) and did it then revert to its previous status of non-person on return to the womb?

What if the baby had died during the surgical procedure? Would he then have acquired personhood for purposes of a death certificate? Suppose the mother changed her mind after the surgery and opted for an abortion, even though she could look forward to a healthy child? That would be legal under current law.

The third case of unraveling logic involves a Texas court case in which a pregnancy center was cited for "deceptive trade practices" and was fined $39,000 for falsely advertising as an abortion clinic, then trying to persuade pregnant women to have their babies. Is this any different from abortion providers who advertise as "women's health clinics" or "Planned Parenthood clinics" in which women are subtly led to the conclusion that abortion is the best option?

I don't think so.

Regardless of how the Court decides the case, the clock is ticking and the day is drawing nearer when killing one's unborn child will again be against the law.

October 19, 1986

FIFTEEN

THE VICTIMS
HAVE THEIR SAY

. . . It is impossible to argue that the consumption of pornography produces no victims.

Since the release of the report by the Attorney General's Commission on Pornography, the White House and Justice Department have received more than eighty thousand letters asking that a strike force be created to implement the commission's twenty-six recommendations. Spokesmen say most of the letters are from individuals and do not appear to part of an organized campaign.

The loudest arguments for doing nothing about pornography have become almost axiomatic: that pornography is "victimless," and that to regulate it would violate the First Amendment.

Is it really "victimless?" Those men who line up in front of the magazine racks at drugstores, or visit the "adult" bookstores, or buy the videocassettes — are they creating thoughts that could cause them to harm someone, or are they just getting their private "jollies" and should be allowed continued access to such materials?

I have obtained some of the letters sent to the White House and Justice Department. After reading them, it is impossible to argue that the consumption of pornography produces no victims.

A California woman wrote: "I have a very personal reason for wanting action to be taken. I was molested by my older brother when I was a child. It all started when he and a friend acquired some pornographic magazines. After looking at and becoming aroused by those pictures (he was thirteen or fourteen years old), he began to explore and experiment on me. Unfortunately, it did not stop with me. I've recently learned that for many years he also explored and experimented with my two sisters and brother. . . ."

A woman in Illinois wrote: "Several years ago, my husband became 'addicted' to pornography. He frequently visited the adult bookstores in our town—watched X-rated pornographic films and bought magazines. This escalated until he started trying everything out on me in our bedroom. I tried to understand that he had a problem, but after one and a half years of fear and three visits to specialists to correct damage he had done to my female organs, I filed for divorce. . . . Considering that my husband is a respected businessman and that no one could tell from looking at him what degrading acts he can do in bed, I'd hate to think what damage pornographic materials are doing to other families."

A youth worker in Washington State wrote that he "sees the effects of pornography on our nation's youth nearly every day. I was a sexually abused child. Pornography was prevalent in our home and, along with any effect it had on my parents, it has had a lasting impact on my relationship with my wife. . . ."

A man in Wisconsin said, "I have never admitted to anyone until now that I was a victim of pornography. As a child I was sexually abused by a father who used pornography. . . . Who will speak for the children who are the innocent victims?"

From a woman in Missouri: "As a child I was molested and abused by adult users of pornography. It left me with a warped sense of what 'love' was about and eroded my self-esteem. The lack of self-esteem stayed with me and I grew up to marry a man who also used pornography. I went through hell being married to him. At first the abuse was mostly emotional, but it soon escalated to physical violence, ending when he tried to shoot me with his rifle. I believe his behavior was directly linked to the pornography he read."

The porn world doesn't care about the people, of course. The Washington, D.C., public relations firm Gray and Company has been contacted by the Council of Periodical Distributors about the possibility of representing the organization in combating the pornography commission's findings. In a letter to John Harrington, executive vice president of the Council for Periodical Distributors, Gray senior vice president Stephen M.

Johnson outlines a strategy that is based entirely on criticism of the commission and its members, rather than confronting its findings or attempting to rebut the testimony of pornography's victims.

Johnson says that Harrington and a media coalition organized to derail the commission's objectives ought to plan on spending between $600,000 and $900,000 during the first year. To an industry that takes in several billion dollars annually, this is peanuts.

September 7, 1986

OUT OF SIGHT, OUT OF MIND

The facts have not changed, only the way of thinking about them.

Since abortion was made legal fourteen years ago, those who favor it have increasingly found themselves in retreat. Technological advances have made growing numbers of Americans uncomfortable with the carnage that has, so far, snuffed out the lives of roughly twenty-one million.

These advances have included spectacular photography that shows life within the mother's womb. It has also provided us with pictures of an actual abortion.

In these ways we have been forced to confront the pain a baby feels during an abortion and the testimony of women who have had abortions and who now say they were duped.

Now the pro-abortionists are advocating the "ultimate" drug, one that not only has the potential for producing abortions at home but also has what some regard as a positive side effect, the anesthetizing of the conscience.

The drug is called RU-486. French researchers who developed it say the drug, depending on when it is taken, either prevents implantation of the developing human embryo or dislodges the embryo from the wall of the uterus after implantation. In either case the developing baby dies when the lining of the uterus starts to slough off, and the woman starts bleeding.

That RU-486 is the answer to the pro-abortion movement's prayers is evident by a number of statements.

Columnist Joan Beck of the *Chicago Tribune* wrote, "The new drug will not only be less traumatic to a pregnant women's body than surgical abortion, it will also be kinder to the conscience.

. . . She can tell herself she is taking the new drug to induce late menstruation. She won't even have to admit to herself that she is getting rid of an early, growing embryo."

Isn't this what George Orwell was talking about when he invented the word "Newthink"? The facts have not changed, only the way of thinking about them. Once again, technology has arrived just in time to allow us to remove ourselves one step further from the consequences of our actions, making tolerable the intolerable.

In a recent response to a letter that decried the beauty of life that an aborted child would miss, "Dear Abby" wrote that there are positive sides to abortion that the writer had missed. By aborting a baby, wrote Abby, the reluctant mother would make sure the child would never know "the pain of poverty, prejudice, a Hiroshima, a holocaust, a nuclear accident. That 'lucky' child [the child who is aborted] will never be terrorized by youth gangs that kill innocent bystanders. It will never fear disease from polluted air or drinking water, or the deadly consequences of playing in a schoolyard unthinkingly located close to a toxic waste dump."

So, because it is impossible to guarantee that the unwanted unborn baby might never be victimized by a youth gang or breathe toxic fumes while playing in a sandbox, it ought to be aborted? This defies reasoned thinking.

RU-486 will be available in France this year. It ought to be rejected in this country by the Food and Drug Administration because of potentially hazardous side effects. It should be rejected, too, because the U.S. has never had a national debate on abortion. It is long past time for that debate, so that the people, not non-elected federal judges, can decide the matter once and for all.

January 4, 1987

SEVENTEEN

UPPING THE
RHETORICAL ANTE

*. . . Government's role should not end with education on how to per-
form homosexual acts safely. It ought to be discouraging the acts themselves for the sake of promoting the general welfare.*

The National Academy of Sciences upped the rhetorical ante
on AIDS last week when it said that the spread of the disease has
become such an urgent problem that a "national health crisis"
exists and if something isn't done to stem its spread, "the present
epidemic could become a catastrophe."

The Academy wants President Reagan to lead the attack
against AIDS. But the Vatican has already taken the highest
leadership road possible. It is telling people to stop doing what
causes AIDS and it is telling bishops and priests not to confuse
compassion for AIDS sufferers with tolerance for the practices
that lead to the disease.

The Vatican statement that, "In 1986 AIDS cannot be ignored
in any consideration of the moral and ethical issues raised by
homosexuality," prompted an angry reaction from spokespersons
for the homosexual community, who said that the church is supposed to be showing compassion and caring for those who suffer
from AIDS instead of furthering "bigotry and hatred."

There is nothing bigoted or hateful in the Vatican warning
against practices that have been shown to spread AIDS. Is it
showing bigotry and hatred against victims of lung cancer, emphysema, and heart disease to label cigarettes as killers, or is it
the highest form of compassion?

True mean-spiritedness is not displayed by those such as the
Vatican when they strongly condemn the practice of homosex-

uality. Rather, it is demonstrated by those who wish to indulge themselves in the very behavior that brought on this national health crisis; behavior that is now leading to the deaths of innocent people.

There is now a real possibility that AIDS could break out of the high-risk groups and attack the general population. If that happens, some members of the general population who have felt safe from the AIDS epidemic may be prompted to respond irrationally.

While all reasonable people must deplore any acts of violence against homosexuals, the Vatican statement correctly assesses the conditions that lead to such behavior: "when civil legislation is introduced to protect behavior to which no one has any conceivable right," people should not be surprised when "irrational and violent reactions increase."

To prevent the spread of AIDS, and its terrible medical and social ramifications, the government must exert stronger leadership. Lesser plagues of the past brought a more direct assault from government than the "kid gloves" approach we have seen taken against the AIDS "catastrophe." In 14th Century Europe during the bubonic plague, the sick, and also those suspected of suffering from the disease, were isolated, not only for their benefit but for the benefit of the uninfected as well. Quarantines were imposed on imported food and visiting foreigners until it was assured they were not contaminated.

During cholera, tuberculosis, and polio epidemics in the United States, similar strict measures were taken. Quarantining persons with AIDS is not necessary because the disease cannot now be contracted through casual contact. But a change in the behavior that is spreading AIDS is clearly indicated. The Surgeon General, that same official who has campaigned aggressively against cigarette smoking, has rightly urged that we educate people about AIDS and the ways to prevent its spread. But government's role should not end with education on how to perform homosexual acts safely. It ought to be discouraging the acts themselves for the sake of promoting the general welfare.

Just as in the 1950s, when polio was the nation's most critical health concern and local and federal health officials acted by closing public swimming pools, so must they now move immediately to close every bath house, bar, and other place where it can be proved that homosexual males engage in anonymous sex and where drug users congregate.

Such an action won't eradicate AIDS, but like labels on cigarette packages, it will send a clear message on the dangers AIDS poses to our nation.

November 6, 1986

EIGHTEEN

ECLIPSE OF REASON

One must wonder . . . if we have political leaders or federal judges who place a higher value on human life than they do on political considerations.

The pro-life movement has a new and awesome weapon in its arsenal. It is a film created by a man who was once an abortionist before he became convinced that what he was doing was wrong.

Dr. Bernard Nathanson, founder of the National Abortion Rights Action League and now a persuasive defender of the unborn, premiered a sequel to his controversial 1985 film, "The Silent Scream," which used sonography to show an actual abortion.

Nathanson's latest work, titled "Eclipse of Reason," was presented at a Washington news conference the same week as the Martin Luther King holiday observance. To underscore what King fought against, the TV networks broadcast twenty-year-old pictures of blacks being beaten and sprayed with powerful water hoses by the police. Those who are not racists must have experienced a sick feeling when exposed to such scenes of inhumanity.

It is that same emotion which "Eclipse of Reason" evokes.

The film is gruesome, gory, and graphic. It is reality, just as those beatings were reality a generation ago.

The color film shows the inside of the womb and the body of a 5-month-old baby. In clear, crisp detail, the viewer observes a hand and then a head. Minutes later this same baby, which had been enjoying tranquility, is dismembered and the head crushed as it is pulled from the womb.

In addition to the stomach-turning reality of abortion, the film exposes ignorance about abortion. In on-the-street interviews, people reveal that they believe the Supreme Court, in its 1973 ruling, allowed abortion only in the first three months of pregnancy. When informed that a woman may have an abortion up until the moment before delivery, for the poorly defined excuse of benefiting her "mental health," those interviewed expressed shock, noting that this should not be allowed because a child is able to survive outside the womb as early as four and a half months after conception.

This film is too powerful to ignore. It is the ultimate persuader for anyone with enough honesty to confront the question it raises. A truly openminded person cannot see it and continue to favor "choice" on abortion.

One must wonder after viewing the film if we have political leaders or federal judges who place a higher value on human life than they do on political considerations. Probably not very many, which is why this film is needed to ignite the fires of outrage.

January 25, 1987

PART TWO

MORE CANDOR
LESS PANDER

NINETEEN

AN EQUAL AND OPPOSITE REACTION

It has been a Supreme Court engaging in "legisprudence" that has brought on profound fundamental change in our society.

One of the basic laws of physics a student is supposed to learn in school is that for every action there is an equal and opposite reaction. The same is often true in politics.

Remarks by Attorney General Edwin Meese that Supreme Court interpretations of the Constitution are not "the supreme law of the land" in the same sense as the Constitution itself set off a firestorm of criticism from those camps that think it is. Meese was denounced by the American Civil Liberties Union as inviting lawlessness.

ACLU executive director Ira Glasser said Meese is "the most dangerous Attorney General in this century." Perhaps Meese is dangerous to legal Lone Rangers like Glasser who have successfully used the federal courts to advance a left-wing agenda that would not have had even a voluntary prayer in the Congress. But Meese stands in the rather proud company of those who have had less than high regard for the Supreme Court's over-inflated image of itself.

The nation's first attorney general, Edmund Randolph, who was probably in the ACLU's opinion, the most "dangerous" attorney general of the eighteenth century, expressed in a 1792 letter to James Madison views similar to Meese's. Referring to a case that dealt with state sovereignty (Georgia vs. Brailsford), Randolph wrote, "In his decision last week, he [Chief Justice John Jay] showed no method, no legal principle and no system of reasoning."

Perhaps the most famous objection to a Supreme Court decision was voiced by President Abraham Lincoln in a speech given in Springfield, Illinois, on June 26, 1858. Referring to the Court's Dred Scott decision declaring black slaves chattel who could be bought and sold because they were not persons within the meaning of the law, Lincoln said, "We think the Dred Scott decision is erroneous. We know the Court that made it has often overruled its own decisions, and we shall do what we can to have it overrule this."

Criticizing critics of the Supreme Court is nothing new, either. In a speech to the 1913 graduating class at Harvard University, Chief Justice Oliver Wendell Holmes said, "The attacks upon this court are merely an expression of the unrest that seems to wonder vaguely whether law and order pay. When the ignorant are taught to doubt, they do not know what they safely may believe." Holmes apparently believed that the Supreme Court expressed the ultimate wisdom and that anyone who questioned the Court's rulings was ignorant.

One can observe similar sentiments expressed in the attacks on Meese. The attorney general did not say, as some of his critics allege, that Americans are free to disregard Supreme Court decisions and become a law unto themselves. What he did say was that, while decisions by the Court "bind the parties in the case and also the executive branch," they are not "binding on all persons and parts of government, HENCEFORTH AND EVERMORE." This should be obvious from such cases as Dred Scott.

A political cartoon by the *Tampa Tribune's* Wayne Stayskal illustrates the conflict between the view that the Court is the supreme authority and the view that it is made up of mortals capable of making mistakes — mistakes that should be corrected. The cartoon shows a man sitting before his television set. A newsperson says, "By a 5-to-4 vote, the Supreme Court today declared itself God." It was the Court's presumption of omnipotence that brought on the criticism by some members of the public and Attorney General Meese.

One of Meese's critics accuses him of trying to bring about a "fundamental change" in the way the Court operates. In a sense this is true, but Meese's reaction was triggered by the Court's habit of making new law instead of interpreting the

Constitution as it was written. Some have called the former practice, "legisprudence," and the latter "jurisprudence."

It has been a Supreme Court engaging in "legisprudence" that has brought on profound fundamental change in our society. The Reagan Administration is seeking to do nothing more radical than return the Court to its Constitutional roots.

November 2, 1986

YESTERDAY, TODAY, AND FOREVER

As the abortion holocaust progresses, we have moved beyond allowing a woman to determine the nature and the value of the child she is carrying.

Remember asking (or being asked) that childhood question, "When is a door not a door?" And the answer is, "When it's a jar!"

Here's another one. When is a human being not a human being? The answer is when he or she is in a womb in Minnesota.

The Minnesota Supreme Court decided by a 6-to-1 vote that a man accused of killing an eight and one half month old unborn baby in an automobile accident cannot be charged with homicide.

The facts of the case are these. A car driven by John Soto of St. Paul collided in November, 1984, with another car driven by Jannet Anne Johnson, who suffered a fractured pelvis and broken leg. Johnson, who was on her way to pick up her husband, was taken to a hospital emergency room where fetal distress signs were detected. Doctors performed a Caesarean section, but the baby was stillborn. An autopsy showed the baby died of head injuries.

How important this case was to the "pro-choicers" became clear when the Minnesota Civil Liberties Union entered the case, not on behalf of the woman or her dead baby, but on behalf of Soto, who was allegedly drunk. The money used to pay Soto's legal expenses came from the Reproductive Freedom Project of the American Civil Liberties Union. What about the "reproductive freedom" of the woman and her husband who wanted their baby?

The problem with the Minnesota law and similar laws in twenty-three states is their inconsistency. At least fifteen other states have laws that make it a crime to interfere intentionally or negligently with a pregnancy. So, where you reside is important, but it is also important whether the baby is in the "right" womb if you want the law to protect your unborn child.

The inconsistencies in the human life debate grow more numerous each year. The Minnesota case was decided as Mothers Against Drunk Driving were concluding their coast-to-coast march to raise public awareness of the cost in human life and suffering from those who drink and drive.

The Minnesota Supreme Court decides a baby is not a human being until it is born, and we read in the same newspapers stories about the effects of PCP on the unborn, or the effect of smoking and alcohol on unborn babies (and the news accounts use the word "babies" in many cases because the presumption is that the woman wants to have a healthy child. If she is going to abort, she probably would not wish to stop drinking and smoking for the baby's sake.)

As the abortion holocaust progresses, we have moved beyond allowing a woman to determine the nature and the value of the child she is carrying. Now the courts say it does not matter what the woman wants. The courts, at least in Minnesota and in nearly half the other states, say you are not human until the day you are born. What are you, then, a car? What about those who survive saline abortions? Are they "human"?

Dr. Ronald Cranford, a neurologist at Hennepin County (Minnesota) Medical Center, offered a new opinion on when the unborn child ought to be able to expect legal protection.

Dr. Cranford was quoted as saying, "Neither conception, birth or viability—the ability to survive outside the womb—ought to be the point at which the fetus obtains protection under the law." He said that ethicists are moving toward an "awareness-of-suffering standard" as the time at which a fetus should be given legal protection. In effect, he said, that standard reflects the ability of a fetus to have a conscious reaction to a stimulus.

That "standard" should prove to be no problem for the "pro-choicers." All they must do is anesthetize the baby prior to aborting it and, viola! So much for any "reaction to a stimulus."

No matter how many scientific, medical, legal, or moral arguments pro-lifers come up with, there are never enough. The reason is that "pro-choicers" are not interested in facts, anymore than heavy smokers need additional information to convince them to stop smoking. It is a matter of the will, not evidence.

Like smoking for women in the 1920s, abortion in the 1980s has become a symbol of liberation. If abortion had emerged as something other than a political issue (like civil rights for blacks with its widely accepted moral overtones), it would have been halted long ago because of the increasing evidence in favor of the unborn.

Like Alabama Governor George Wallace, who once stood in the schoolhouse door and said, "Segregation today; segregation tomorrow; segregation forever," his modern-day equivalents (those who would deny the unborn their civil rights) stand in the abortion clinic door and say that no matter what evidence is presented, no matter how many homes for women with crisis pregnancies are established, it will still be, "abortion yesterday, abortion forever."

December 12, 1985

NO MORE BOGEYMEN

Why shouldn't the pigeons have an atheist target along with all the others?

Nearly twenty-five years after sending shock waves through Middle America with her Supreme Court case that outlawed mandatory prayers in public schools, atheist leader Madalyn Murray O'Hair, perhaps the most famous three-named person since John Wilkes Booth, has resigned as head of the organization she founded, American Atheists.

In her typical feisty manner, O'Hair told the group's sixteenth annual meeting in Somerset, N.J., that she wasn't retiring and she certainly was not withdrawing from "the fight," but that she wants to "step aside for the new upcoming generation" of atheists. It is a small group, what with a Gallup Poll finding more than 95 percent of Americans believe in God, but O'Hair is nothing if not undeterred.

Demonstrating that humility is something else in which she does not believe, the sixty-seven-year-old O'Hair said she still thinks there should be a statue of herself "in every park in America" as recognition of her twenty-four-year struggle to gain respect for atheists.

I agree. Why shouldn't the pigeons have an atheist target along with all the others?

Proving that she has no intention of mellowing, O'Hair let loose some verbal blasts at people she thinks are stupid enough to believe in anything higher than their own minds.

"Anyone who is praying is in fantasyland. Life after death, gods, angels, and goblins: that is all fantasyland. Atheists deal only with reality.

"Agnostics (those who doubt the existence of God) are simply gutless atheists."

"Anyone who believes in the virgin birth of Christ and Reaganomics is irrational." David Stockman, call her office. You're at least halfway there.

I first met O'Hair more than ten years ago on a news panel program in Houston. I asked her, grandmotherly type that she is, why so many people appear threatened by her.

She responded, "I'll tell you why I think some religious people are afraid of me. It is because some of them are not sure of what they believe. If they were sure, I would be no threat at all."

My second encounter with O'Hair was less pleasant. At Dartmouth College four years ago, where I was delivering a speech, she came in and mistook me for someone she obviously disliked. She proceeded to curse at me loudly in front of the entire audience. The students were not impressed by her lack of manners.

In most families children who find God are thought well of, but just the opposite was true in the O'Hair household. Her son Jon, who is taking over for his mother, "kept the faith" so to speak. But older son Bill was converted and wrote a book, *My Life Without God*, in which he severely trashed his mother for ruining his early life and for what he says were her sympathies toward Communism. Murray relates how she attempted to gain Soviet citizenship but was refused because, according to Murray, she did not have a job. Murray said the Soviet authorities told his mother, "We don't have welfare here like you do in America."

Bill Murray was subsequently ostracized by his mother. Though the two live less than two hundred miles apart in Texas, they have not spoken to each other in years.

By the way, the O'Hair resignation deals the most serious of blows to fundraisers, who have had a field day for a generation raising money for various causes by using the specter of Madalyn Murray O'Hair's taking religion off the airwaves, or removing "In God We Trust" from our money, or denying Congress the right to hire chaplains to say prayers before meetings of the House and Senate.

In fact, the past twelve months have not been good ones for conservative fund raisers. First, Ted Kennedy said he would not run for President. Now Madalyn Murray O'Hair resigns as president of American Atheists. If this keeps up, there won't be any more bogeymen to kick around.

I don't know whether Madalyn Murray O'Hair will ever get a statue of herself in every park, or even in only one park, but I do believe she should have her own national holiday for all she has done to America.

The day I recommend is April first.

April 27, 1986

TWENTY - TWO

NOT WILD
ABOUT HARRY

Day, me-say-day, me-say-day, me-say-day-ay-ay-oh. Daylight come and me wanna go home. . . .

Singer Harry Belafonte, who is known in the world of hyphenations as an "activist-entertainer," is said to be seriously considering a run for the Democratic nomination for the U.S. Senate from New York. If he wins the nomination, his opponent will be incumbent Republican Alfonse D'Amato.

Bill Cosby is leading a stampede of one on Belafonte's behalf.

After a lengthy meeting with Belafonte, New York State Democratic chairman Lawrence Kirwan gushed, "He has long been committed to an enlightened foreign and domestic policy. What I find most impressive is his grasp of the issues."

Really?

Let's consider how "enlightened" Belafonte's views are and how firmly he grasps the issues.

"Day-oh . . . day-ay-ay-oh. Daylight come and me wanna go home. . . ."

In a July, 1983, speech at the National Press Club, Belafonte ripped into U.S. policy in Latin America and the Caribbean.

Belafonte said that the United States has "taken away democracy where it existed and institutionalized dictatorships" in Latin America.

"Day, me-say-day, me-say-day, me-say-day-ay-ay-oh. Daylight come and me wanna go home. . . ."

On the subject of the now liberated Grenada, where he made the movie "Island in the Sun" twenty-six years earlier, Belafonte said, "This country [the U.S.] would have been much richer in our future efforts if we had made friends with [then Grenadian President] Maurice Bishop and assisted him in his programs."

Has Belafonte read the documents captured by American troops which tell of plans by Bishop's New Jewel Movement, underway at the time of the invasion, to shut down Grenadian churches, silence the press, and use the country as another of Castro's revolutionary staging areas?

"Come Mr. Tallyman, tally me banana. . . ."

Warming to the subject, Belafonte delivered the standard leftist apology for all Communist dictators. It's called the "Officer Krupke excuse": They is depraved on account of they was deprived of U.S. aid. According to Belafonte, the U.S. made a mistake by not backing Fidel Castro's revolution in Cuba and drove him to the Soviet orbit after he took power in 1959.

"If I were oppressed in any of these countries," said Belafonte, "and had come to this country seeking assistance and aid, and had gotten the kind of treatment that most of these countries are getting, I too would join the Communist Party. I too would take up arms against an oppressive society."

"It's six foot, seven foot, eight foot bunch. . . ."

Belafonte concluded his view of what constitutes an "enlightened foreign policy" by again demonstrating his "grasp of the issues": "If we had befriended Fidel Castro when he came here three weeks after marching into Havana, if the people . . . in Washington had dealt with him with dignity and some sense of fair play, we would not be in the crisis we are in today. We spread communism around the world more than Communists could ever hope to do."

There you go again, Harry. You always blame America first, just like those "San Francisco Democrats." How did the U.S. help spread communism in Eastern Europe? Is it America's fault that the Soviets are practicing genocide against the Afghan people?

Three months after his press club speech, in October, 1983, Belafonte performed in East Berlin at a "World Peace Concert" sponsored by the East German Communist youth organization, whose slogan for the event was "Away with NATO's rocket decision." Propaganda themes were flashed on giant screens, ascribing the roots of world evil to American foreign policy.

Does this stuff represent the "new" Democratic Party we

were promised after the 1984 election? Is this the philosophy the Democratic leadership believes will lead to a majority in the Senate this fall and capturing the White House in 1988?

In the immortal words of Stan Freberg, who recorded a parody of Belafonte's "Banana Boat Song," "It's too piercing, man, it's too piercing."

March 2, 1986

TWENTY-THREE

ACQUIRED INTEGRITY DEFICIENCY SYNDROME

Be honest, now. When someone mentions the word "handicap," do you think of an AIDS sufferer?

The chief human rights officer for the state of Florida has ruled that AIDS is a handicap and that discrimination against its victims is illegal. The ruling came in a case involving a Broward County employee who was fired after he contracted the deadly disease.

We should have been able to forecast this ruling when in 1976 attempts were made to amend the Rehabilitation Act to specify that only "traditional handicaps" would qualify for federal anti-discrimination protection. Those attempts failed.

The Act was amended in 1978 to specify that an alcoholic or drug addict could be fired only if his addiction interfered with his ability to perform work. I was surprised to learn that drug addiction and alcoholism are regarded as handicaps.

Be honest, now. When someone mentions the word "handicap," do you think of an AIDS sufferer as fitting into the category? I usually think of persons in wheelchairs or on crutches, or persons who are blind or mentally retarded, or who suffer from other disabilities either because of an accident, a combat-related injury, or a condition they developed through no fault of their own.

Doesn't the first letter of the AIDS acronym stand for "acquired"? And how is it acquired? Through what we used to call "illicit" sexual intercourse before everything became "licit," and through intravenous drug use.

The decision by the human rights chief in Florida came during the same week that a judge threw out a lawsuit against the R. J. Reynolds tobacco company. The suit was brought by a man who claimed the company was liable for making a product that injured him. Not so, said the judge. There were ample warnings concerning the health hazards of tobacco use and the man smoked at his own risk.

It is the same with AIDS. Can there be anyone who does not know by now how AIDS is acquired? We have witnessed one of the biggest media blitzes in history on the subject.

If AIDS is to be classified as a handicap — with all of the job protection such a designation implies — why not designate more traditional venereal diseases, including syphilis and gonorrhea, as handicaps also? After all, they have been around a lot longer than AIDS. Why discriminate?

Now that AIDS victims are considered handicapped, at least in Florida (and in New York where a similar ruling has been issued), will they qualify for those special license plates and be allowed to park closer to shops, restaurants, and public buildings than the rest of us?

It seems all one needs nowadays to gain government approval of what used to be the natural consequence of unnatural behavior is to belong to a constituency large enough to attract television cameras and to put fear into spineless politicians who are afraid to say no to anything that can vote.

The human rights officer in Florida has been afflicted with a much more common disease: acquired INTEGRITY deficiency syndrome.

December 19, 1985

TWENTY-FOUR

BACKS AGAINST
THE WALL

Planned Parenthood and its friends in Congress and the press are con-ducting a major disinformation campaign.

The National Family Planning and Reproductive Health Association, Inc. (NFPRHA), one of Planned Parenthood's products of conception, has delivered a press release about the importance of an upcoming House Appropriations Committee vote on an amendment that would prohibit federal funds from going to organizations that perform or counsel women to have abortions. The release says that if pro-abortion forces are not successful in defeating the amendment by Representative Jack Kemp (R-New York) to Title X of the Public Health Service Act, then "the game is over."

Kemp and his Senate colleague, Orrin Hatch (R-Utah), want Congress to reaffirm its intention for Title X, first enacted in 1970, that public money is to be used to provide contraceptive services to indigent persons and not for abortion. Kemp says he wants to rebuild "the wall of separation between contraception and abortion."

More than $146 million is involved in Title X, but politically the stakes are much higher.

The NFPRHA is not using apocalyptic terms solely for the purpose of persuading people to write out a check, as is usually the case with pronouncements from both Left and Right. They know their backs are against the abortion clinic wall.

In the abortion debate, momentum is everything. In 1973, the pro-abortionists were at their zenith. Since then, medical and political momentum has clearly shifted in the direction of the pro-lifers.

Planned Parenthood maintains that it does not perform abortions. What it does, however, is refer women to clinics it operates, which make up the nation's largest abortion network. Some eighty seven thousand abortions were performed last year at clinics owned and operated by Planned Parenthood. The organization received an estimated $17 million in fees for such "services."

And what does this money buy?

Melanie Lockhard knows. She counsels women in crisis pregnancy situations in Virginia. Increasingly, she is seeing women who exhibit "post-abortion trauma."

Lockhard says that in recent months she has counseled eighty women who had first visited a Planned Parenthood clinic. She says only five of the women told her that Planned Parenthood presented the options of keeping the baby or placing it for adoption. In the other seventy-five cases, abortion was presented as the wisest and virtually only alternative.

Planned Parenthood, she says, also engages in rhetorical sleights of hand by employing such euphemisms as "contents of the uterus," "the mass of tissue," and "product of conception," instead of "baby" or even "fetus" when talking to pregnant women about their options. Lockhard says the women tell her that nearly all of Planned Parenthood's counseling is done in groups of eight to ten and there is little opportunity for the one-on-one encounters that might produce a result other than abortion. Lockhard says one young woman was told by a Planned Parenthood counselor that up until the second month of pregnancy there is nothing present but a placenta.

Another example of your tax dollars at work.

The proposed amendment to Title X would prohibit its funds from going to "any organization that provides to any pregnant woman abortion procedures, counseling for abortion procedures, or referral for abortion procedures, unless the life of such woman would be endangered by carrying the fetus to term."

Planned Parenthood and its friends in Congress and the press are conducting a major disinformation campaign about Title X. They say the organization does not spend Title X funds on abortions. And they falsely contend that programs designed to reduce unwanted pregnancies through contraception will be cut if the amendment passes, resulting in more unwanted pregnancies and more abortions.

It is difficult to follow this logic since the amendment would not restrict contraceptive counseling. But as I say, when your back is against the wall and some of your fellow soldiers predict that if the amendment succeeds, the game is over, you say desperate things.

November 10, 1985

TWENTY-FIVE

FOLLOW THE LEADER

. . . There is a Grand Canyon-sized chasm between what the rank-and-file thinks and what their "leadership" says they think.

If a prophet is to be without honor in his own country, then vindication is the next best thing he can hope for. If this was Clarence M. Pendleton's hope, it has now been fulfilled with the publication of a new study comparing the views of black leaders to the rank and file.

Pendleton, the chairman of the U.S. Civil Rights Commission, has been the target of substantial criticism for saying last November that black leaders are responsible for leading blacks into "a political Jonestown." As expected, much of the black leadership turned their guns on Pendleton.

Now comes the study by the Center for Media and Public Affairs, a nonprofit, privately funded research group, which shows that at least on some of the issues we have been led to believe are of utmost importance to blacks generally, there is a Grand Canyon-sized chasm between what the rank and file thinks and what their "leadership" says they think. In fact, it might be fair to suggest that rank and file blacks are not just marching to a different drummer, they are part of another parade.

On the issue of affirmative action, which the Justice Department has been trying to eliminate and the National Association for the Advancement of Colored People has been trying to keep, a whopping 77 percent of rank-and-file blacks reject the concept, while 77 percent of their "leadership" wants to retain it for jobs and college entry.

On the issue of forced busing to achieve numerical balance among the races in public schools, 68 percent of the leaders favor it, while 53 percent of the rank and file oppose it.

Only 14 percent of black leaders want to prohibit all abortions, while 43 percent of blacks generally oppose the procedure.

Prayer in public schools? Forty percent of black leaders don't want it; 83 percent of the black community, about the national average, do want it.

I spoke with Pendleton about the survey. He said that, yes, he does feel somewhat vindicated. "Someone has heard my pleas," he said. "We all don't think alike."

Pendleton said that black leaders, including himself, have no monopoly on black thought. He blamed the press for being unfair to the black community by uncritically approaching certain preordained "leaders" and speaking only to them. Without a controversy between blacks and whites, he said, the press cannot make any money. "There is no money in writing about harmony."

Pendleton said most blacks oppose affirmative action because they know they will always wonder about their abilities and whether they made it on merit or for other reasons. "Preferential treatment means you want somebody to hold your hand," said Pendleton. "The only thing I want is for someone to hold the door open."

Pendleton likes to tell the story of Eddie Robinson, the football coach at Grambling, one of the best known black colleges in the country. Robinson tells his players they are as much Americans as anyone else, and they have to compete for positions. Pendleton said Robinson decided in 1960 to be "Eddie Robinson, the American" and not part of the "them and us battle."

Recently "NBC Nightly News" aired a series called "Facing the Bitter Reality." The series examined the growing debate over whether government programs designed to help blacks have done as much (if not more) harm than good. The fact that this is being debated so hotly is evidence, I think, that these programs have at the very least achieved far less than was predicted or expected, and that the only alternative is again to encourage individual initiative and a return to traditional family life along with a rejuvenation of the once-powerful black church. (Pendleton said that since government got in the way, and people have forgotten how to tithe.)

Of course, this would mean that the black "leadership" might have to find another line of work. It might be fun to see what sorts of jobs some of them would choose.

September 26, 1985

TWENTY-SIX

HUMANE TREATMENT

. . . Otherwise good-hearted, sensible people are quick to anthropo-morphize animal pain and shut themselves off to the human fetus who is subject to far more agonizing torment.

You may think that the most powerful lobby in the country is one of the following: unions, feminists, civil rights advocates, homosexuals, the right wing, big oil, or the auto industry. You are wrong. The most powerful lobby in the country is the animal lobby.

After only a four-day sit-in at the National Institutes of Health in Bethesda, Maryland, "animal rights activists" persuaded Health and Human Services Secretary Margaret Heckler to suspend the use of federal funds for brain-trauma experiments on monkeys at a University of Pennsylvania head injury clinic.

The protesters carried signs that said "stop animal agony." They provided the networks with a videotape of animals said to be suffering from such experiments. A spokesperson described the tape as the animal rights equivalent of the pro-human life film, "The Silent Scream."

In ordering the cutoff of funds for the procedures, which were designed to help doctors treat human head injuries, Secretary Heckler said, "The use of animals must occur under protected and humane conditions. . . ."

The word humane is defined as "marked by compassion, sympathy, or consideration for other human beings or animals." But far more compassion, sympathy, and consideration are being offered to animals than to unborn babies, whose lives continue to be snuffed out at the rate of one and a half million per year.

"The Silent Scream" shows a baby, not animals, writhing in pain. The networks conducted selected interviews with doctors who have a professional and/or political interest in maintaining the abortion status quo. These doctors called the film a fraud and claimed that the fetus depicted was only responding to stimuli, not real pain. Anyway, they said, the choice ought to be left up to a woman and her doctor.

Why, then, where animals are concerned, can't the choice be left up to the people who stand to benefit from such experiments and their doctors? Why do arguments in favor of humane treatment for animals bring instant results from otherwise slow to act government officials, while similar appeals on behalf of humans fall on deaf ears?

Two years ago when the Defense Department announced plans to shoot dogs to study ways in which the wounds of human soldiers might be better treated on the battlefield, pickets appeared outside the home of Secretary Caspar Weinberger. The following day the planned experiments were called off. Appeals for other animals and their "rights" have come from those speaking for whales, seals, bald eagles, horses, elephants, goats, and even kangaroos, to say nothing of the now famous snail darter. Action has followed in most cases. But it is always open season on the unborn and no "bag limit" is imposed.

Dr. Bernard Nathanson, the former abortionist who co-produced "The Silent Scream," says the Left has been egregiously inconsistent in the entire abortion issue. "In the case of animals," he say, "the question is isolated in its crystal purity. There are no women's rights, no feminism, nothing else. You have an animal suffering pain. Period. If only people could see unborn babies in an identical crystal form without the politics."

Nathanson says he is astounded that otherwise good-hearted, sensible people are quick to anthropomorphize animal pain and shut themselves off to the human fetus who is subject to far more agonizing torment.

The inconsistencies are incredible. Animals are mistreated, but babies are not. Animals suffer excruciating pain, but some pro-abortion doctors, who have far less evidence to support their view than pro-life doctors have to support theirs, say aborted babies do not.

What would happen if the "pro-choice" arguments were used in the animal rights debate?

—No one is forcing you to give up your pet for a head-crushing experiment, so why don't you stop imposing your morality on others? Besides, an animal is not human (even if we allegedly descended from them).

—There are too many animals and the population needs to be reduced.

—There are too many unwanted and abused animals and one way to cut down on animal abuse is to kill more of them.

—Every animal should be a wanted animal.

What would happen is that the person making these arguments would be visited by animal rights demonstrators who would occupy his living room or office.

Nat Hentoff of the *Village Voice* put it succinctly when he told me, "If only the pro-choice Left could think of the fetus as a baby seal in utero." If we are really all animals anyway, and there is nothing to distinguish humans or give them special value, why are some animals more equal than others?

July 28, 1985

TWENTY-SEVEN

NEW AND IMPROVED NEWSPEAK

A tramp is still a tramp. A Communist is still a Communist, the rewritten Oxford dictionary notwithstanding.

The Soviet leadership is a couple of years late, but they have finally done something to mark the year 1984 and the best-selling book by the same name. Just when the world thought it was safe to go back into the sea of semantics, the Soviets have shown what a prophet George Orwell was by rewriting the *Oxford English Dictionary* so that words such as "communism," "imperialism," and "Fascism" are defined in ways favorable to Soviet political goals instead of reflecting the true meanings of the words.

But wait. They are not alone. At a time when, as William Safire has noted, there has been "a salutary reaction against the use of euphemisms," certain liberal Democrats, masquerading as "progressives" or "pragmatic progressives," as New York Governor Mario Cuomo calls himself, are engaging in a new round of "newspeak" of their own.

Senator Edward M. Kennedy (D-Mass.) started it by saying in a speech at Hofstra University that his party must search for "new approaches" (not new ideas, you understand; that was Gary Hart's line) to the needs of the country.

"One thing is certain," said Kennedy, "we cannot and should not depend on higher tax revenues to roll in and redeem every costly program. Those of us who care about domestic progress must do more with less."

Kennedy is hardly a born-again supply-sider, nor is he ready to sing "Amazing Grace" ("I once was blind, but now I see"). The test will come when he suggests who is going to have to do more with less. Let's see him stand up to the demonstrators if he suggests cutting welfare or reducing funding for Planned Parenthood or tightening immigration laws or any of a host of other issues near and dear to liberal hearts. If he says no to the groups to which he has previously pandered, then we can be convinced he has "seen the light," but not before.

Kennedy and the Soviets have a lot of company as they forge new euphemisms out of real definitions.

The *Wall Street Journal* reports that some women politicians are backing away from the feminist label to expand their base of support. Do they still favor abortion and the ERA? Of course, but they are no longer as up front about it, preferring to speak instead about "families." Ask them to define what a family is, however, and you quickly discover that these people are still lost in the woods with the rest of the special interests.

My favorite story about euphemisms comes from an interview more than ten years ago in the now defunct *Washington Star.* Xaviera Hollander, author of *The Happy Hooker*, was interviewed by a female reporter. After a number of statements touting the supposed joys of the new sexual freedom and how much Hollander said she liked being a prostitute, the reporter asked her, "What is the difference between you and what my mother used to call a tramp?" Hollander was unable to reply.

A tramp is still a tramp. A Communist is still a Communist, the rewritten Oxford dictionary notwithstanding. A liberal is still a liberal (in his heart, you know he's left).

If liberal Democrats, like Ted Kennedy, are going to indulge in euphemisms, the rest of us are going to need a glossary so we can tell what is really being said. In order to prepare properly for this new wave of euphemisms, I have written a glossary of liberal terms so that you can know how they think and be better prepared to translate the "new newspeak," which even now is being written deep within the bowels of Democratic National Headquarters. Here are some samples:

Tolerant: a person who is willing to accept any form of behavior, because there is no standard for right and wrong (other than in Central America).

Diversity: a close relative of tolerance. If you are tolerant, then you can appreciate diversity, such as homosexuals, adulterers, rock and roll lovers, wife beaters, etc.

First Amendment: that part of the Constitution which protects liberals so that they may publish, write, or broadcast anything they wish. No such amendment is available to conservatives, who may wish to see their values reflected in textbooks or the media.

Pluralism: the process whereby one gives in to a liberal when there is a disagreement. The process does not work in reverse. If one tries, he is antipluralistic.

Dark Ages: that period in history to which conservatives wish to return us. (Have some fun by asking a liberal for the centuries that made up the Dark Ages and then ask him to recite what he believes to have been the horrors of that period.)

There's more, but you get the idea.

A wise man once advised against putting new wine into old wineskins. The same advice holds true for new ideas in old pools. Besides, you can't put anything new into a container until the old is emptied. The so-called "new approaches" are nothing more than a lot of hooey.

April 14, 1985

TWENTY-EIGHT

EVOLUTION AND THE LAW

If judges invoke only a subjective and contemporary view of the law, free of even minimal absolutes, we are left with the most potent threat to our liberties that can be imagined.

Supreme Court Justice William J. Brennan, Jr. delivered a speech last weekend at Georgetown University in Washington that revealed, better than any other modern address, the underlying cause of the nation's legal turmoil during the past thirty years.

Most Americans have been led to believe, in their history classes and through press reports of Supreme Court rulings, that legal findings were rooted in a type of pathological examination of the brain tissue of the Framers of the Constitution.

Brennan believes that justices are to interpret the Constitution, not on the basis of any absolute, unchanging moral code, but rather "as twentieth-century Americans." He said, "We look to the intervening history of interpretation. But the ultimate question must be: What do the words of the text mean in our time?"

Brennan said that the Constitution "rests not in any static meaning it might have had in a world that is dead and gone, but in the adaptability of its great principles to cope with the current problems and current needs."

This is nothing short of evolutionary law. Man evolved from monkeys. The law evolved at the same time. Man is not unique, because man arrived on the scene by pure chance. The law is a product of man's imaginings without a unique beginning.

As Chief Justice Charles Evans Hughes remarked in 1907, "The Constitution is what the judges say it is." No standard. No absolute. No "inalienable rights endowed by our Creator." Only what an elite corps of justices believes to be true at a given point in history (even though they may have no basis for that truth other than what the "community's interpretation" of truth is at that moment).

What is truth? According to Justice Oliver Wendell Holmes, truth is "the majority vote of that nation that could lick all others."

Holmes, in his work *The Common Law* (1881), which laid the basis for the undermining of the common law, believed that the law is not logic but experience. (Brennan echoed Holmes when he argued for an "adaptable" Constitution.) According to Holmes, the law was the product of man's opinion, supported by the absolute rights of the majority.

As Constitutional lawyer John Whitehead points out in his book *The Second American Revolution*, Holmes wanted the principles of common law, which had guided courts and governments for centuries before America was settled, to be left in the dust of history for the concept of evolving law. Again, Brennan echoed Holmes when he stated, "Those who would restrict claims of right to the values of 1789 specifically articulated in the Constitution turn a blind eye to social progress and eschew adaptation of overarching principles to changes of social circumstance."

Yet it was precisely because the Framers believed in the PRINCIPLE that all men are created equal, that the law ultimately reflected that absolute. Had equality been an idea that appeared as a blip on an evolutionary screen, blacks might still be plucking cotton on the white man's plantation.

The Constitution is not rootless, as William B. Ball has noted. Ball, who frequently argues church-state cases before the Supreme Court, says that the Constitution must govern our judges, not the reverse. Otherwise we have a government of men and not of laws.

If judges invoke only a subjective and contemporary view of the law, free of even minimal absolutes, we are left with the most potent threat to our liberties that can be imagined.

Chiseled into the marble of Thomas Jefferson's memorial in Washington are these words: "God who gave us life gave us liberty." Can the liberties of a nation be secure when we have removed a conviction that these liberties are the gift of God?

Justice Brennan says that efforts by the Reagan Administration to the return the law to a foundation of immutable principles is "arrogance cloaked as humility." On the contrary. The real arrogance is displayed by judges who feel that all truth resides in their heads and that they are not to be taught either by the lessons of history or by "Nature's God."

The problem will not be solved solely by replacing liberals with conservative judges on this and on lower courts if the new judges mirror the old in their belief in the doctrine of evolutionary law which is taught in most of the top law schools. So it will not be enough to change the top without doing something about the bottom. But we must begin somewhere and nominating justices to the Supreme Court who believe that law originated outside a monkey's head is a good start.

October 17, 1985

EROSION

Those who said the ushering in of abortion on demand would never lead to infanticide and euthanasia made such a mistake.

It is not often that one is able to witness the effects of soil erosion all at once. The slide of a coastline into the sea is a slow process, requiring many years. Once in a while, though, a hurricane comes along and a process that would normally take a decade or more occurs within hours.

The same can be true in matters having to do with moral erosion, involving paramount concerns such as life and death. A storm occurred last week and when it had ended, it was obvious how far the moral shoreline had eroded.

When Roe vs. Wade ushered in abortion on demand in 1973, proponents laughed when critics predicted that infanticide and euthanasia would closely follow. "Impossible," they assured them. "Crazy," they labeled them.

Two incidents in the same week demonstrate who the crazy ones really are and just how possible and even probable the twin horrors of infanticide and euthanasia have become.

Horror 1: Infanticide. Two dozen "severely handicapped" infants allegedly were allowed to die without surgery at the Oklahoma City Children's Memorial Hospital because they flunked a test printed in the *American Academy of Pediatrics* magazine. The formula determines the "quality of life" by multiplying the infant's physical and mental condition by the anticipated "contribution from home and family and the contribution of society."

In a letter sent to the hospital by the American Civil Liberties Union and organizations for retarded and disabled people, a class-action lawsuit was threatened unless the hospital changes the policy.

The letter said that "depending on the team's assessment of
the 'contributions' from home and society, one child may be
recommended for life-saving surgery while another, with identical physical prognosis, may be recommended for death."

Horror 2: Euthanasia. Roswell Gilbert was convicted of
shooting to death his ailing wife in Ft. Lauderdale in what was
described as a "mercy killing." Said Gilbert, "I know it's murder,
but so what? Some things are more important than the law."

Hilda Waxman, a retired nurse, was quoted by *USA Today* as
saying, "Euthanasia decisions should be intellectual, rather than
emotional, by uninvolved persons."

Betty Bertoldi told the same newspaper, "I believe in mercy
killings. The old should be given the dignity of dying gracefully."
Being shot in the head is graceful?

What is so surprising about all of this? Once it has been determined that there is such a thing as a human life not worthy to
be lived, it is only a matter of time before rules are established
that fix some lives as more valuable than others and require
those making such decisions to be guided by some shifting standard other than the Jeffersonian one, which speaks of life as an
inalienable right "endowed by our Creator." If Jefferson had only
known that references to the Deity in the 1980s would be deemed
unconstitutional!

Any "normal" person could have seen this coming. The Associated Press reported eight years ago that a British doctor, John
Goundry, said that a "death pill" will be available and perhaps
obligatory by the end of the century. He said that doctors should
be able to give a "demise pill" to old people if they ask for it. He
also said, "In the end I can see the state taking over and insisting
on euthanasia." One can hear the echo of the Gestapo boots
coming down the hospital corridor while the modern-day rock
hit "Another One Bites the Dust" plays over the Muzak system.

Swedish public health physician Ragnar Toss wants to open
a suicide clinic for the more than two thousand Swedes who kill
themselves each year—"not to treat them but to help them do
it." Writing in the *Swedish Medical Journal* in August, 1977, Dr.
Toss said that this suggestion is related to the choice women have
on abortion.

Biomedical "ethicist" Peter Singer has compared handicapped infants to dogs and pigs who are devoid of any superior position when it comes to making life and death decisions.

One mark of an honest person is that when he has made a mistake, he admits his error. Those who said the ushering in of abortion on demand would never lead to infanticide and euthanasia made such a mistake. Now that they have been proved wrong, those criticized are waiting for them to demonstrate their integrity. Meanwhile, the killing continues.

May 16, 1985

THIRTY

A READY-MADE ISSUE

Communism is an equal-opportunity oppressor. It discriminates against everyone.

A white prison guard brings Nelson Mandela, the South African black, a Coca-Cola as he prepares for his first interview by journalists in eight years. John Lofton of the *Washington Times* and I watch Mandela take the soft drink from a small tray. Whether he appreciates the irony of the moment, I cannot say. He accepts the drink without looking at the guard, as if the role reversal were his due.

In some ways, it is his due. After twenty-one years in prison, Nelson Mandela displays none of the characteristics, including resignation to one's fate, of other prisoners I have met who are serving life terms. But why should he? Mandela is the focus of international attention. He leads his revolution in a time-honored way; from behind prison walls. He is the eye of a gathering political hurricane that swirls around him. It may be that he is more effective in prison than out, more effective to "the revolution" as an unseen symbol than as a visible one. There is a sense in which he relishes the attention he receives, though his visitors are restricted and his mail is censored.

As Robert Stroud was "the Birdman of Alcatraz" because of his devotion to birds, so Nelson Mandela might be called the Botanist of Pollsmoor Prison, because of the small garden he keeps in one of the prison hallways. Spinach, brussel sprouts, onions, and cauliflower grow inside oil drums that have been sliced in half lengthwise. It appears that the special favor has been granted to him alone. No other hobbies can be seen in the immaculate prison.

After we write down our names and the names of our publications on a sheet of paper he provides, Mandela asks me if I know Senator Edward Kennedy. When I tell him I do, he brightens and asks me to convey his warm regards to the senator, who was not allowed to see Mandela during his visit to South Africa earlier this year.

Perhaps Mandela took us for liberals. I can think of no other reason why he would be so candid in his remarks unless, at the age of sixty-seven, he believes he has nothing to lose.

Mandela looks good. His tall, slim body appears accustomed to the green prison suit. His dark hair is flecked with gray, as if he had just come in from a snowstorm. His skin is the color of leather. A deep crease divides his upper from his lower forehead. Otherwise his face is unlined. His last interviewer, attorney Sam Dash, wrote in the *New York Times Magazine* last winter that Mandela seemed to him to resemble a "head of state." My own impression is of someone far less grand.

Speaking slowly so that a verbatim transcript can be made of his remarks (we were not allowed to tape-record the interview), Mandela acknowledges that State President P. W. Botha is right when he says that Mandela would again resort to armed violence should he be released. Mandela says he would be back in prison within twenty-four hours after he is set free because he would again engage in the terrorist acts that landed him in prison in 1964. He also states he believes that communism would be "better" than the current situation in South Africa, because "communism has no color bar." He is partially right. Communism is an equal-opportunity oppressor. It discriminates against everyone.

Mandela's assertion that he is not a Communist rings hollow. He says only that he has been "influenced" by the teachings of Marx. That, of course, is what Fidel Castro said before he came to power. Ditto for Commandante Ortega in Nicaragua. But if it walks like a duck and talks like a duck and has feathers like a duck, then it's a duck. If Mandela is not a Communist, then Marx was a misunderstood capitalist.

I can only speculate why John Lofton and I succeeded in interviewing Mandela when other journalists have been denied access to one who may now be the world's most famous prisoner. Perhaps the government hoped Mandela would hang himself. If that was their motive for granting permission for the interview, they were not disappointed.

The *Johannesburg Star* published the interview on its front page. Since remarks by Mandela are banned, it took special permission from the top to print his comments in South Africa.

Mandela's words can only strengthen the government's case against clemency for him unless he agrees to renounce violence. They also make points for the government against those who are marching this week for Mandela's unconditional release. And they ought to cause some concern for the 180 American congressmen and thirteen senators who signed a resolution last year asking that Mandela be freed. They have given their opponents in the next election a ready-made campaign issue. Who wants to be labeled "pro-terrorist"?

August 29, 1985

THIRTY-ONE

WARNING SIGNS

The Left failed because it watered down its message in favor of a method. Now, the Right risks falling into the same trap.

Warning signs, be they for cancer or for economic problems, are best heeded when they first appear, lest they lead to undesirable ends. Warning signs have begun to appear for the Right, which it will ignore at its own peril.

Contemporary conservatism was born in 1979, following a lengthy gestation period. Its catalyst and chief architect was what came to be known as the Religious Right. The Left made a fool of itself by denouncing religious conservatives for meddling in what had, until then, been their exclusive territory.

Now, less than a decade later, the Right is in danger of making many of the Left's mistakes and causing similar damage to itself. Chief among these mistakes is looking to government as a first resource instead of a last resort. Whereas the Left has looked to government exclusively to impose its social agenda, the Right now flirts with the same heresy.

There is an advertisement for a bank at Washington's National Airport that says, "Welcome to the most important city in the world." The ad seems pretentious until you realize that Washington IS the most important city in the world. The reason, of course, is that Washington stands for power, and it is the use of and desire for power that is the city's fuel.

In Washington at the 43rd annual convention of National Religious Broadcasters (NRB) one observes two kinds of power side by side, not necessarily coexisting but more often struggling for supremacy. It has nothing to do with church and state, with God and government. It is far more subtle than that. A press re-

lease proclaims "famous names appearing at NRB convention."
Is there no room for the meek and lowly?

Listening to the questions of reporters in the hotel lobby, one
senses that the warning signs are at the critical level. Here,
among mostly decent men and women concerned with the spiritual welfare of the world's population, there are few questions
about that welfare. Questions, instead, center on who is favored
among the delegates to lead one of the kingdoms of this world in
the 1988 election.

The convention program reflects the growing influence of
politics in the Church (yes, I said politics in the Church, not
the Church in politics). Pictures of White House Communica-
tions Director Patrick Buchanan, President Ronald Reagan,
Vice President George Bush, and Jeane Kirkpatrick, along
with religious-political hybrids such as the Rev. Jesse Jackson (a
once and probably future presidential candidate) and the Rev.
Pat Robertson (probably a future one), fit snugly next to those of
religious leaders.

Some elements of the Religious Right have already nomi-
nated and elected George Bush as the next President. This is
curious, not only because none of its leaders appears to have had
a serious discussion with Bush as to why his pro-abortion and
pro-ERA views have changed and what brought about his "conversion" on two of the Right's most important litmus tests, but
also because Robertson would seem far closer to the religious
and political agenda of the Right than Episcopal layman Bush.

If, as some have suggested, Bush's transformation was for
purely pragmatic reasons, is the endorsement of him by some of
the Religious Right any less so? It is a poor negotiator who en-
dorses a candidate before bargains are struck.

The danger in all of this blurring of distinctions between
temporal and eternal power has never been to the state. It has
always been to the Church. If the Church appears to be nothing
more than a ratifying body for the policies of secular authorities,
then the Kingdom of God risks being perceived as the kingdom
of this world and thus loses its distinction. If the leaders of the
Religious Right feel they cannot or must not ever criticize the
secular authorities for fear of being denied access to them, then
they have become nothing more than a tool of the state, which

has always sought to use religion to bless its own agenda.

The Left failed because it watered down its message in favor of a method. Now, the Right risks falling into the same trap.

Having spent five years within the bowels of the Religious Right, I speak with some authority and knowledge of the pitfalls the pursuit of power and influence can bring. The Church violates no canon or constitution when it registers voters and speaks out on moral issues, but it also should remember to Whom it belongs. And no Bridegroom likes a bride that commits adultery.

February 9, 1986

THIRTY-TWO

THE MISSING
WEAK LINK

*Many of SDI's critics on the Left would put more faith in Soviet
promises . . . than in American technology and the assurances of our
leaders. There is a message in this somewhere.*

If you watched the television coverage of the Challenger disaster long enough and read the liberal columnists, you could tell
that the critics of the President's proposed Strategic Defense Initiative thought they had at last found a weak link in the chain.
The "anchorpersons" first suggested that the apparent defect in
the solid rocket booster was evidence that a far more sophisticated and intricate system, on which we would literally bet our
lives, had no chance of working properly.

The *Washington Post's* usually glum columnist Mary McGrory
quickly picked up the theme when she wrote: "The President
must consider that 'Star Wars,' a space-based program, is the
ultimate in the high technology that failed the Challenger. Its
premise is that millions of gadgets, with hairline timing, will
function flawlessly on computer command—when missiles
start flying."

Such arguments are more flawed than whatever it was that
led to Challenger's explosion.

Again, it appears from preliminary evidence that what failed
may not have been "high tech" at all, but the booster system
that had worked flawlessly during twenty-four previous shuttle
launches. Besides, SDI is not a manned program. The system
can be placed into orbit on unmanned boosters and, should one
or more boosters fail, all that would be necessary is for another

system to be sent up. SDI would not become fully operational until all systems were in orbit.

The apparent failure of the Challenger booster doomed that mission and the astronauts who were on board. While the Challenger accident may have delayed some SDI experiments, there is no reason to believe it proves the space defense system cannot work.

Once SDI is finally in orbit, the satellites would become as stable as any others have been. As most recently demonstrated by Voyager, satellites, unlike home appliances, often exceed their life expectancies. If Voyager had failed to send back pictures of the planet Uranus, no one would say, "Let's not send another probe."

Retired General Daniel Graham of the Washington think tank High Frontier, who is widely regarded as the architect and driving force behind what is officially known as SDI, but derisively referred to by critics as "Star Wars," tells me that he believes there should be many individual satellites using available technology, which would be capable of defending the United States, rather than a few highly sophisticated ones, which he says have a greater potential to malfunction.

In any case, Graham predicts that arguments against a space-based defense system linked to the Challenger incident (which, not surprisingly, included criticism of SDI from the Soviet disinformation organ *Pravda*) will disappear in less than two weeks. Besides, he says, a twenty-four out of twenty-five success record on a booster rocket is not bad. And the tests of SDI, so far, seem to have gone very well indeed. Graham does not believe the Soviets would launch waves of nuclear salvos, hoping that one of every twenty-five might get through.

It is peculiar when you think about it. Many of SDI's critics on the Left would put more faith in Soviet promises about disarmament and nuclear freezes and supposed desires for peace (are you listening, Afghanistan?) than in American technology and the assurances of our leaders. There is a message in this somewhere.

February 6, 1986

THIRTY-THREE

DOES ANYONE KNOW WHERE NICARAGUA IS?

Perhaps our own Congress could benefit from some lessons in geography and history.

Of all the arguments used against President Reagan's request for $100 million in aid to the Nicaraguan rebels, probably the silliest was that "most people don't know where Nicaragua is." This might have evoked an impassioned response from our nation's schoolteachers, had many of them not been busy taking competency tests.

Maybe the critics of the President's aid request are right. A survey by a University of Miami geography professor two years ago found that 42 percent of the students thought the Falkland Islands were off the coast of England. Fewer than half the students could find Chicago on a blank U.S. map, and 8 percent did not know where Miami was.

Studies at Marquette University and the University of Wisconsin show similar ignorance of geography, with some students placing Poland where China should be.

Last fall, a study funded by the National Endowment for the Humanities found that many American high school seniors also have a poor background in history. One-third could not identify Winston Churchill or Josef Stalin; two-thirds failed to put the Civil War in the correct half-century; one-third did not know that the Declaration of Independence was signed between 1750 and 1800, and one-half could not tell in what half-century World War I occurred.

Perhaps our own Congress could benefit from some lessons in geography and history. The President was criticized for attempting to educate his critics in these subjects during a March 16 television address. Opponents of his aid request laughed when he showed maps of Central and South America turning red. Perhaps he should have started with Estonia and Latvia and moved through Eastern Europe and on to Asia and Africa. There might have been less laughter by the time he got to our hemisphere.

Members of Congress ought to be assigned to watch a TV "documentary" on the Communist apologist Anna Louise Strong, now making the round of public television stations.

Writing about the film, called "Witness to Revolution," *New York Times* critic John Corry said that the work represents "history turned upside down" and is something that "spreads disinformation."

"How does nonsense like this get promulgated?" he asks of the film, which is about a woman "who never met a left-wing dictator she didn't like."

Omitted from the film is Strong's greatest fiction; her comment on the Soviet GULAGs: "The labor camps have won a big reputation throughout the Soviet Union as places where tens of thousands of men have been reclaimed. So well known and effective is the Soviet method of remaking human beings that criminals occasionally now apply to be admitted."

Corry said this kind of propaganda won't subvert anyone, "but it does suggest that a great many people have lost their critical faculties." Which is precisely what has happened in the debate on Nicaragua.

Opponents of the president have resurrected the ghost of Joe McCarthy. While McCarthy's methods were wrong, his warning that communism is dangerous was correct. McCarthy was the best thing that ever happened to communism. Because of McCarthy, many are afraid to warn of the dangers of this political disease for fear of being accused of using "McCarthy-like tactics."

There are two levels to this debate over aid to Nicaragua. One level asserts that communism is an ever-expanding force that will not rest until it dominates the world. The other level says that while communism is a serious threat, it does not threaten the U.S. in Nicaragua.

It is precisely at this point that one wishes the President's opponents could be pinned down as to what constitutes a threat. Certainly not an attack on Miami. A lot of people don't know where Miami is, remember?

Representative Thomas Foley, the Democratic whip, said on ABC's "This Week With David Brinkley" that he would vote for aid to the rebels if the Soviets introduced just one MIG fighter. And what would Foley then do? He says he would support the President in whatever the President wanted to do, short of dropping a nuclear bomb. Yet when the President wants to do the minimal thing now, Foley won't support him. He says he doesn't want to fight a "proxy war." But isn't that precisely what the Soviets, Cubans, PLO, Red Brigade, and Libya are fighting in Nicaragua?

Instead of questioning the patriotism of some members of Congress who oppose the President's aid request, someone should give them a test on history and geography.

March 27, 1986

BETTER DEAD
THAN COED

The view that one person's discrimination is another person's equal opportunity, or that one person's guerrilla is another's freedom fighter, is not unique.

Few things in life are more delicious than discovering hypocrisy among a class of people who delight in pointing out such tendencies in others. And so, not even the dessert of fresh strawberries with whipped cream was as sweet as the story in the paper about Goucher College's decision to end a 101-year-old tradition and admit men to the heretofore all-women school.

Declining enrollment and declining interest in all-women's colleges were cited as the main reasons for the decision to admit men to the school in Towson, Maryland. What interested me far more than the reasoning behind the decision was the reaction by some students opposed to the move.

About 125 of the students protested the decision by wearing T-shirts that read, "Better Dead Than Coed." They surrounded the alumnae hall where the board of directors was about to vote and chanted loudly, "Men are not the answer." Other students painted "No men" in block letters on their forearms.

Press treatment of the protesting students was sympathetic and straightforward. Contrast this with the coverage and editorializing one might expect had Goucher been an all-male school that had barred women students for 101 years.

Or, what about an all-male club that, for whatever reasons, did not wish to admit women? This was the case until recently at the National Press Club in Washington. The Cosmos Club, an exclusive male preserve along Washington's embassy row, remains so today in spite of scathing editorials, protests, and unfavorable publicity.

Imagine, and this is not hard to do because it used to be the way things were, an all-white school or club barring blacks and saying that "integration is not the answer." One can still hear the echo of Alabama Governor George C. Wallace's ringing pledge, "segregation today, segregation tomorrow, segregation forever."

Sexism, the reasoning of some goes, is so ingrained in our culture that the best way to educate young women and to encourage them to be strong and independent is to place them in an intellectual convent, at least as far as the classroom is concerned. One protesting Goucher student observed, "In a coed school, the guys talk more in class. (I thought that the talkative women was a stereotype created by men.) They're called on more in class. They are the leaders. Just because it's 1986, doesn't mean we are equal."

I am not insensitive to the charge that some women are still discriminated against because of their gender, but I fail to see how one can be taught equality in an unequal environment. It is the same argument that is made about quotas. In order to be equal, minorities must create a system that is inherently unequal.

The view that one person's discrimination is another person's equal opportunity, or that one person's guerrilla is another's freedom fighter, is not limited to Goucher or to academia.

The Reverend Jesse Jackson launches a boycott against CBS because he says it employs too few blacks and no one calls him a censor. That label is reserved for those who boycotted 7-Eleven because it carried, until just recently, magazines that employed too many naked women.

Three Mile Island has a nuclear power plant meltdown and demonstrators take to the streets. A movie, starring Jane Fonda, is made. But where are Jane and her friends in the aftermath of the Chernobyl "disaster?" Working on the next exercise videotape, no doubt.

The list is endless and includes criticism of the U.S. for having a handful of military advisers in Central America, but not a discouraging word at all for the thousands of Cuban troops in the region; and international silence about occupied

Afghanistan, but liberal outrage over the U.S. liberation and non-occupation of Grenada.

At Goucher, perhaps the starkest contrast of all was that while students demonstrated in favor of sexual apartheid in Towson, students at Dartmouth, Brown, U.C. Berkeley, and other prestigious schools demonstrated against racial apartheid in South Africa.

As the saying goes, "You've come a long way, baby."

May 15, 1986

THIRTY-FIVE

WHAT LADY LIBERTY IS ALL ABOUT

. . . Patriotism used to be commonplace, like dog biting man. Now, patriotism is in the "man bites dog" category.

One month before the celebration to end all celebrations, marking the 100th anniversary of the Statue of Liberty, an eleven-year-old Vietnamese refugee, whose family is on welfare, summarized more than the fireworks, more than the show biz, what the Lady in New York Harbor is all about.

Hue Cao, who spoke her native Vietnamese and a Chinese dialect but no English when she fled Vietnam with her mother and two brothers seven years ago, is a celebrity in Honolulu, not only because she won a state-sponsored essay contest on "What the Statue of Liberty Means to Me," but also because the prize of a new car threatened to disqualify her mother from receiving welfare benefits. The car was sold and the proceeds placed in an educational fund for Hue. Someone else donated to the family a car that was worth one dollar less than the maximum allowed under welfare benefits.

Hue's sentiments about her adopted home would be treated cynically by those who are embarrassed by expressions of patriotism, were it not for her genuine innocence and honesty. Indeed, Hue says things about America that we used to take for granted but now consider news, which suggests that we have acquired a patriotism deficiency syndrome.

"We wanted to live in America, a land where there is liberty and justice," said Hue in her essay. "Every time we saw a picture of the Statue of Liberty, my mother would tell us SHE is America. America is a place that lends a hand to those in need.

The Americans care for all people, from hopeless to homeless people. . . ."

Remember, this was written before the car, before the recognition, and obviously, before anyone told Hue about the uncaring Reagan administration, which supposedly hates the hopeless and homeless. Funny how those who do not drink from the media well sometimes see more clearly than habitual watchers of the evening news and other sophisticates.

Hue is a press agent's dream. At a news conference in which the Hawaiian congressional delegation served as a prop, Hue thanked her teacher, her fellow students, and especially the principal "for allowing me to go places during school hours." She even thanked the press! Talk about disarming. Show me a reporter who could be cynical after facing a child with no guile.

On June 9, Hue Cao and her family will apply for citizenship in their new country. She awaits word from producer David Wolper whether her essay will be read during the national celebration in New York, July 4 weekend. She has already received a call from President Reagan.

The downside of this story is that patriotism used to be commonplace, like dog biting man. Someone saying something nice about America was not news. Now patriotism is in the "man bites dog" category, and that ought to tell us how far we have to go toward shamelessness in openly expressing our love for this country, the popularity of "Rambo" notwithstanding.

Hue Cao's essay also contains a lesson for those who believe it is possible to negotiate successfully with Communists: "After the Vietnam War ended, the Communists took over and they were very cruel, stern, and ill-tempered. They took away our freedom, and worst of all, they could kill anyone. We had a very hard life under them."

Hue Cao and her family are part of that "wretched refuse" from a "teeming shore," part of the "tempest-tossed" beside which the Lady lifts her lamp to help them find their way through the Golden Door. She is the latest in a long line of people who will feel a special something on July 4 weekend that natives cannot experience.

June 8, 1986

THIRTY-SIX

FREEDOM-MINDED CITIZENS

In the war in Nicaragua, one side is forced to abide by the rules, while the other side gets to make up its rules as it goes along.

What concerns me most about the uproar over the recent downing of a C-123K cargo plane in southern Nicaragua is the double standard applied to the incident by some liberals in Congress and the press.

In the war in Nicaragua, one side (the freedom fighters and the United States) is forced to abide by the rules, while the other side (the Sandinistas, Soviet Union, and Cuba) gets to make up its rules as it goes along. One army is allowed to receive help from outside, but the other army may receive none. It does not take a genius to predict the inevitable outcome of such a conflict.

There are suggestions in the United States that whoever is behind the funding of such U.S. civilians as Eugene Hasenfus, the pilot and sole survivor of the downed plane who is now on trial in Nicaragua, ought to be forced to abide by "the rules" and be barred from giving similar aid in the future. Meanwhile the Soviet Union, directly and through various proxies, gives unrestricted financial and military support.

Thus far, the Soviets and Cubans have supplied the Sandinistas with more than one hundred T-55 tanks (Somosa's National Guard had only three U.S. tanks), nearly thirty PT-76 light amphibious tanks, 340 armored vehicles, seventy-five fuel tankers, more than seventy long-range artillery pieces and multiple rocket launchers, and more than thirty helicopters — including the world's fastest attack helicopter, the Mi-24/HIND D.

Such disparity between U.S. and Soviet aid in Nicaragua

makes me think that the "Hands Off Nicaragua" bumper sticker I recently saw on a Washington, D.C., automobile might have been better placed on a Soviet car in Moscow. Unless this inequality is redressed, another nation will fall permanently under Soviet domination.

The Reagan Administration ought not be ashamed of its goal in Nicaragua, any more than the Soviet Union is ashamed of its goal in all of Central America and the rest of the world. The Soviets, without apology and without the handicap of a reluctant legislature and critical press, pursue their objective of world domination. Unfortunately, as regards Nicaragua, their cause has sometimes been assisted by U.S. editorial writers, several members of Congress, and the liberal clergy.

Any U.S. aid, whether government or private, is viewed by such persons as destabilizing. It is destabilizing, all right. It destabilizes the ability of the Soviets and their Cuban and Sandinista comrades to achieve their goals.

As John Norton Moore, professor of International Law at the University of Virginia, counts it, the Soviet Union's chief disciple in our hemisphere, Fidel Castro, has directed insurgencies against seventeen Latin American nations since he seized power in Cuba twenty-seven years ago. Now he is helping the Sandinista government, which has built an active duty and reserve army of more than 100,000 men, compared to only about 22,000 soldiers in neighboring Honduras.

Those who fault U.S. policy for "driving the Sandinista regime into the arms of Moscow" should remember that Commandante Ortega accepted American aid during the last year of the Carter Administration. He then lied to the Senate Foreign Relations Committee when he denied that he and his colleagues had been trained by Castro. Then, to prove his duplicity, Ortega signed multiple agreements in Cuba and Moscow, linking him on paper to the Soviet bloc.

The State Department conservatively estimates that Eastern European economic aid to the Sandinista regime amounts to about $500 million annually. But some people, including former *La Prensa* editor Humberto Belli, say a more accurate figure would be $2 billion.

Congress meanwhile grudgingly authorizes a measly $100

million in non-military aid to the contras. Some wish to do away with even this pittance, allowing the anti-Sandinista forces to twist slowly in the wind. Such a move would invite the Soviets and Cubans to solidify their revolutionary base in Central America and next focus their attention on Mexico.

How many more nations must fall before American liberals realize that communists are deadly earnest about accomplishing their expansionist goals? How many reruns of the communist plan for subverting nations must we experience before some editorial writers and columnists at influential newspapers wake up to the threat inching ever closer to our own borders?

Private American aid to Nicaraguan freedom fighters would not be necessary if Congress had the fortitude to do what is necessary to prevent another communist base from taking firm root in this hemisphere. Until then, it's nice to know there are still a few private Americans who are willing to take a firm stand in defense of freedom.

October 21, 1986

THIRTY-SEVEN

MORAL COMPLEXITIES AND POLITICAL SIMPLICITIES

. . . The withdrawal of U.S. companies from South Africa will hurt South African blacks far more than whites.

Sometimes it takes the shock of surprise to teach us something and when it does, it usually means the situation was far more complex than we had originally thought.

Take the cases of General Motors' withdrawal from South Africa and Bishop John Walker's counter-campaign to keep American businesses active in that African nation.

Most people were surprised when GM Chairman Robert B. Smith announced his company was pulling out of South Africa because of continued economic losses and the sluggishness in ending apartheid. Big business is supposed to be insensitive to such non-economic things as civil rights, the skeptics thought.

Equally surprising has been the personal campaign by the Episcopal Bishop of Washington, D.C., John T. Walker, to persuade U.S. corporations to remain in South Africa. When a respected black leader like Walker, whose anti-apartheid and civil rights credentials are as good as anyone's, favors a course of action opposed by those who proudly consider themselves liberals, it makes one ask what Walker sees that the others have missed.

Walker believes that U.S. companies, rather than pulling out of South Africa and leaving that country to the winds of war, should provide more training for their black South African employees. His is a pragmatic approach to South Africa's problems—an approach he believes would lay the groundwork for a

peaceful transition to majority rule and avoid an economic collapse and its devastating effects on the nation's blacks.

But pragmatism apparently does not interest certain liberal
politicians and other self-styled American spokesmen for South
Africa's non-whites. As Walker puts it, "I don't see why liberals
think there's only one way of going about accomplishing what
you want to accomplish."

The bishop's position has prompted the concern of Randall
Robinson, executive director of a lobbying group, Transafrica,
that believes the best way to deal with the South Africa problem
is to employ economic sanctions that will bring the Pretoria government to its knees. When asked about General Motors' decision, Robinson said he doubted it would have much impact. "It's
quite unbelievable to me that you could expect these companies
to do anything but cosmetic stuff," he said. A pullout by GM is
far from cosmetic, however.

General Motors and other American companies, notably
Mobil Oil, have established excellent records in hiring and helping non-whites in South Africa. According to the Industrial
Publishing Corporation's *Great Achievement* magazine, the auto-
maker was already complying with the so-called "Sullivan Principles"—designed to increase the number of non-white employees working for U.S. firms in South Africa—when it signed the
principles agreement in 1977.

Of a total South African work force exceeding 3,300, 62
percent of GM's employees are non-white. GM also joined with
other companies to provide $1.6 million to establish New
Brighton Technical College, the first institution of its kind in a
black urban area. New Brighton teaches blacks a variety of job
skills.

It is difficult to believe that this company's decision to withdraw from South Africa will not have a definite effect on the
advancement of the nation's non-whites. And that is why such
people as Bishop Walker believe that the withdrawal of U.S.
companies from South Africa will hurt South African blacks far
more than whites.

The bishop's clear and pragmatic thinking on this issue is
the stuff of true leadership. We could apply his approach to
other areas of domestic and foreign policy, but we haven't.

Perhaps that's because too many politicians are habitually running for reelection and find it easier to address issues in simplistic ways, rather than sorting out their complex and far-reaching implications.

October 26, 1986

THIRTY - EIGHT

IMPOSING MORALITY

If elimination of the death penalty is "an idea whose time has come," poll-takers will certainly register surprise.

Five men, convicted by a jury of their peers and sentenced to death according to the laws of the State of New Mexico, had their sentences commuted to life in prison last week by outgoing Governor Tony Anaya, a longtime foe of capital punishment.

This runs counter to two "principles" self-appointed guardians of the Constitution have drummed into us.

The first is that one's personal beliefs must not influence how one administers the law. For example, one may be personally opposed to abortion, but one must uphold the law allowing the procedure for women who want it.

The second is that God must never be brought into a political argument, because that violates the First Amendment's mandate against the entanglement of church and state.

In his commutation order, Governor Anaya has failed to uphold both "principles." The governor said, "My personal beliefs do not allow me to permit the execution of an individual in the name of the state."

Imagine the governor making such a statement about abortion and issuing an executive order to prohibit any more of them in New Mexico. There would be a stampede into federal court to invalidate the order and editorial writers would excoriate him for attempting to impose his personal beliefs on those who do not share them.

The governor also said, "Capital punishment is inhumane, immoral, anti-God, and incompatible with an enlightened society." Continuing the religious theme, he added, "It is my prayer that New Mexico can become the birthplace of an idea whose time has come — the elimination of the death penalty once and for all and the establishment of, and commitment to, a moral, just, and effective criminal justice system in its place."

If elimination of the death penalty is "an idea whose time has come," poll-takers will certainly register surprise. They consistently report that at least three-quarters of the American people favor capital punishment.

As to the death penalty being "anti-God," theologian Dr. Carl Henry tells me that the primary reason for capital punishment is that murder is an offense against God because it is the killing of an innocent human being made in God's image. Christ, notes Dr. Henry, told the Apostle Peter, "He who lives by the sword shall die by the sword" (Matthew 26:52), thereby implicitly upholding the practice of "whoever sheds man's blood, by man shall his blood be shed" (Genesis 9:6). At his Crucifixion, Christ had an ideal platform from which to denounce capital punishment. He did not.

Governor Anaya has failed to understand that capital punishment is a legitimate penalty for an act that is "inhumane, immoral, and anti-God" and for which there can be no other appropriate penalty. Perhaps if life sentences were truly for life he might receive a more sympathetic hearing for his views on capital punishment. The five New Mexico men whose sentences the governor commuted will eventually be eligible for parole.

One of them was convicted of raping and strangling an eighty-year-old woman. The others committed equally heinous acts. Commuting their sentences has cheapened the lives of these innocent victims and made a mockery out of the criminal justice system.

When Governor Anaya was sworn into office, he pledged to uphold the laws of his state. In this instance, he has failed to do so and set a bad precedent, which his successor, Governor-elect Garry Carruthers, has correctly pledged to reverse.

December 4, 1986

THIRTY-NINE

TURNING THE TABLES

Asserting that conservatives are trying to use the courts to pursue their objectives falls into the "look who's talking" category.

Of all the post-mortems performed on the midterm election, the most ridiculous was offered by soon-to-be-former California Supreme Court Chief Justice Rose Elizabeth Bird.

Following her decisive defeat at the polls — she and her two other liberal justices were the first to be removed from that state's Supreme Court by voters since 1934 — Bird blamed the loss on the Reagan Administration, which, she said, had found that "by appointing people to work your will," it could reshape the federal judiciary and achieve through court decisions objectives not achieved in Congress.

Just whose will is she talking about? Did former California Governor Jerry Brown not expect Bird to work her will when he named her to the bench? She certainly wasn't working the people's will by overturning all sixty-one of the death sentences that came before her. Had she forgotten that the Preamble to the Constitution establishes the preeminence of "we the people," not "we the judges"?

Asserting that conservatives are trying to use the courts to pursue their objectives falls into the "look who's talking" category. Ramming a leftist social agenda through the courts and bypassing the legislative branch has always been a tactic of the Left.

Bird also said she expected her defeat to encourage interest groups to attempt to impose their will in the thirty-nine states that have judicial elections. Let us hope that she is correct, since the people are the largest "interest group." A strong dose of their will would be welcome after the force-feeding of judicial activism, which has too often resembled a raw and unchecked power accountable only at election time.

All judges bring their unique personal perspective to the law, just as a physician brings certain personal techniques to surgery. But the physician must accept some truths about the working of the human body, or the patient will die. If judges do not accept certain truths about the law, the law will die, too, and will be buried in a sea of distrust and disrespect that can only lead to anarchy and chaos.

A growing segment of the country feels about the courts the way it does about the television commentators who appear following a presidential speech to tell us what we have just heard and what the president "really" said and meant. They want the law the way it was enacted; not the way someone changes it to fit his or her own perspective.

They are disgusted that dangerous criminals are walking the streets or are not being penalized by laws passed to deter crime and protect the innocent. They are venting their disgust at the ballot box, voting against those they feel have deprived them of the protection of the law.

Bird took a page from 1984 Democratic vice presidential candidate Geraldine Ferraro when she said she may write a book "about the life of a woman in a male-dominated institution." This is the second verse of the "blame America first" tune.

Bird lost the election, not because she is a woman but because she did not serve the law and the people. She thought the law and the people were HER servants.

November 11, 1986

PART THREE

DOUBLE-SPEAK'S TROUBLE STREAK

FORTY

BIGOTRY'S FINAL FRONTIER

Christian parents . . . are stereotyped as Southern rednecks, clad in polyester suits and white socks, who drive pickup trucks with a Confederate flag and a gun rack in the back, chew gum, and are overweight.

A short while ago, the *Washington Post* carried a highly unusual column by Executive Editor Benjamin C. Bradlee apologizing to the city's blacks.

The *Post's* Sunday magazine had offended certain blacks both by publishing a long story on black criminals and by the absence of any blacks in its advertising pages in the premier issue a few weeks earlier. Bradlee's apology followed a demonstration by more than four hundred people who gathered outside the *Post* building. Among the demonstrators was Representative Walter Fauntroy (D-D.C.), who called on the crowd to "boycott negative media" that stereotype blacks as "thieves and robbers and drug addicts."

Post columnist Dorothy Gilliam weighed in with this observation on her paper's actions: "As members of the Washington community, any article that is insensitive to any part of the community offends us all. . . ."

Any part except one, conservative Christians. There is a disturbing undertone of bigotry in the types of things that are being said in print and in court about conservative Christians. If such things were said about any other group, it would produce the type of demonstration (and the type of apology) seen at the *Washington Post*.

Take the court case in Mobile, Alabama, in which six hundred conservative Christian parents are arguing that the Mobile

County schools are violating the First Amendment rights of their children. Their suit contends that dozens of history and social studies textbooks omit the role of Christianity and other religions in American society.

The parents are not asking that ideas and books be removed, only that their point of view be added. When blacks, feminists, homosexuals, and other groups make such arguments, they do so on the grounds of pluralism and academic freedom. When conservative Christians ask to be let in the same door, however, they are branded censors.

The objection to religion in Mobile schools is so strong, say the parents, that one textbook even fails to mention the involvement of black churches in the civil rights battles of the 1960s. It's as if Martin Luther King, Jr., led a totally secular movement with no religious underpinnings or moral force.

Judith Krug of the American Library Association says the Mobile case and similar cases are about "whose values are going to be taught, the parents' or the state's."

Clearly the values of the secular elite have failed. One need only look at the drug abuse, unwanted pregnancy, and illiteracy rates as proof. Five percent of young adults lack basic reading skills and 20 percent lack intermediate skills, according to Rudolf Flesch, author of *Why Johnny Can't Read.*

Recently it was reported that nine New York City high schools have state-paid programs to dispense contraceptives in schools or affiliated clinics, and California schools are instituting similar programs. This demonstrates the failure of valueless sex education.

Yet with all of this proof and more, taxpaying, conservative Christian parents who complain that the state's values have failed and who argue for some of their own values and ideas to be included in the curriculum are stereotyped as Southern rednecks, clad in polyester suits and white socks, who drive pickup trucks with a Confederate flag and a gun rack in the back, chew gum, and are overweight.

Then there is the matter of the Rev. Pat Robertson. Can the press be fair to him? Most commentators discussing the possibility of his running for President focus on his faith, frequently denigrating it, rather than on his position on issues. For example, did *Time* magazine's Hugh Sidney cross the line between fair comment and bigotry when he wrote of Robertson that "he will be ultimately laughed off the stage with his religious vaudeville"? Would Sidney have written the same of an Orthodox Jewish candidate or a practicing Catholic?

It seems that we have a dilemma. On the one hand, a secularized society has been unable to preserve the values it once cherished. On the other hand, to return to those values means accepting ideas that do not meet the test of being "popular" with the press and the secular elite.

October 12, 1986

FORTY-ONE

BACK IN THE CLOSET

It is a slander to suggest that only privatized (and therefore irrelevant) religion is to be tolerated in an otherwise "free" society.

It was only a matter of time before those who want religion put back in the closet where homosexuals used to be would link up between recent terrorist activity in the Middle East with excesses by a few persons in the United States who claim to be acting in the name of God.

First came U.S. District Judge Alexander Harvey II, who while sentencing a man convicted in the bombing of abortion clinics (the man suggested that God told him to do it), compared the acts with "religious extremism throughout the world."

Columnist Carl Rowan picked up on the theme and wrote approvingly of what Henry Clay told the House of Representatives in 1818: "All religions united with government are more or less inimical to liberty. All separated from government are compatible with liberty."

Rowan sees a connection between Islamic extremism in Iran and what he regards as threats to church-state separation in the U.S.

Anyone who does not understand the distinction between Iran's theocracy, based on a flawed view of the Koran, and the republican form of government of the United States, not founded on race or blood, but on ideas rooted in the Judeo-Christian ethic, is not only a poor student of history but is suspect of grinding his prejudicial ax.

Do some commit grotesque acts in the name of religion? Yes. But that is not the fault of religion and it is no excuse for keeping the religious person "in his place."

Did some blacks during the civil rights movement resort to

violence? Yes. But that was no excuse for denying all blacks their civil rights.

For each atrocity committed in the name of religion, thousands of atrocities have been committed in the name of atheism.

In this century alone, examples abound. During the 1930s, the Spanish civil war began when anti-clerics engaged in the wholesale slaughter of Catholic priests, nuns, and brothers. Seven thousand clergy were killed and between twenty-five thousand and fifty thousand lay people died because they were Catholics.

At the other end of the European continent, Josef Stalin, as great an atheist as ever lived, was busy eradicating up to seven million Ukrainians in a forced famine. The brutality of Soviet rule reduced the population in Estonia by 25 percent between 1939 and 1945.

In July, 1970, then House Minority Leader Gerald Ford said, "My heart cries out when I think of how, with one stroke of the pen, Russian laws became immediately effective in all of Lithuania, how the Soviets substituted their entire way of life for that of the Lithuanians and swept away all of their modes of living, how they banned the teaching of religion from school curricula and dismissed the chaplains from the army and the prisons, how they shut down the faculty of theology and philosophy at Kaunas University, expelled the monks, and branded all members of the clergy as enemies of the people."

During China's Cultural Revolution the country went on a wild rampage of hate and irrationality in which millions were unjustly imprisoned or murdered. Add to this the Khmer Rouge atrocities in Cambodia, the killing of Misquito Indians by the Communist Sandinista regime in Nicaragua, and the terrorist acts in El Salvador. Why are these incidents, far more numerous and far more costly in human lives than supposed religiously-based "terrorism," never cited by the self-appointed "guardians" of our liberties in the judiciary and on the editorial pages?

Worldwide communism, at its core atheistic, has killed an estimated 140 million people since 1917.

Millions upon millions of people attend churches, synagogues, and mosques around the world and practice their faith without resorting to violence.

It's a slander to suggest that only privatized (and therefore ir-relevant) religion is to be tolerated in an otherwise "free" society.

It is the autonomy of man, not the authority of God, that leads to most of the world's ill. Jean-Jacques Rousseau, por-trayed by the late historians Will and Ariel Durant as the most important influence on modern thought, believed in the total au-tonomy of man, free from any restraints by the state or the church. Rousseau's writings were adopted by Robespierre in the Reign of Terror in eighteenth-century France. The church was viewed as the enemy of the state and many clerics perished under the guillotine.

So, if we are to play the game started by Judge Harvey and Carl Rowan, listing what they regard as incidents of religious extremism, let us also develop a parallel list of religious in-tolerance and atheistic terrorism.

A fair-minded person would have to conclude that a system based on the autonomy of man ("We have no king but Caesar") has wreaked far more havoc than systems based on mutual ac-countability to a power higher than the state ("We hold these truths to be self-evident: that all men are created equal and are endowed by their Creator with certain inalienable rights . . ."). The list would include on the debit side the crazies who are now running Iran and dismembering Lebanon and still take up less than a page, while the other column might be turned into a small book.

July 21, 1985

FORTY - TWO

AS IF IT
NEVER HAPPENED

The press would be more comfortable with a crusade led by a representative of Pontius Pilate . . . than it is with one led by Billy Graham.

The local television stations considered these stories more important than the opening night of the Greater Washington Billy Graham Crusade: an apartment fire (no injuries); a shopping center fire (no injuries); a car in the river; a terrorist killing; a local suicide; Reagan in Hawaii talking to Marcos; a Christmas-in-April project; a bubble festival; weather and sports.

One station carried a ten-second blip that reported Graham was in town and that he hoped to attract 140,000 people. It did not mention that the Vice President of the United States was there along with twenty-one thousand other people on opening night. It said nothing of the purpose of the Crusade.

The TV station that did use sound had a clip of George Bush welcoming everybody to Washington and one of Graham saying there were more people there than in Madison Square Garden. But the people had not come to set attendance records or to hear the Vice President.

Coverage like this (and virtually no coverage at all in succeeding days) is why so many Christians distrust the press. They have observed press sensitivity toward ethnic and racial minorities, homosexuals, abortion-providers, pornographers, and all sorts of outrageous behavior. They have seen the press follow the Baghwan Shree Rajneesh to the uttermost parts of the earth. But when it is "their turn" and they think their morals and world view deserve some attention, they see insensitivity and a kind of censorship by omission of anything resembling spirituality.

So there are press reports on Graham's view of nuclear weapons, his relationships with former presidents (and the current one), biographical material . . . anything so as not to have to deal with what really makes Graham who and what he is: a preacher of the Gospel.

In South Africa there is continued conflict between blacks and whites. At the Graham Crusade in Washington, blacks and whites (and Orientals and Hispanics) sit together and embrace one another. News is conflict in South Africa, not resolution in Washington.

It is fair to ask whether the press is so taken by conflict that it refuses to see solutions. But then by ignoring Graham, the press does not have to confront such uncomfortable philosophies as truth. After all, how could ratings be maintained and papers sold if a solution to humankind's most pressing problem, alienation, was discovered?

The press would be more comfortable with a crusade led by a representative of Pontius Pilate ("What is truth?") than it is with one led by Billy Graham ("Neither communism nor capitalism is going to win the world. The Kingdom of God is going to win the world").

On the second night of the Crusade there are no television cameras. It is as if this were a play. Opening night gets some reviews, but night number two, and succeeding nights, will be the same, so why bother to go again?

Why is this? How many other creeds have produced so many people who proclaim a common and life-changing event that has transformed their lives? From the poorest and least powerful to the richest and most powerful, what other force has touched each end of the spectrum and every class of person in between?

Three years ago, Wayne Valis resigned his position as special assistant to the President. In a statement, Valis said, "I've come to believe, especially after my time with Reagan, that there is no ultimate solution to human problems. Every solution that you find contains the seeds of other human problems. . . . Hopefully you can trade more vexing problems for less vexing problems." That is the catechism of Washington and, indeed, much of American life. Billy Graham came to the city to offer another way. Too bad he was virtually ignored.

There is another minister who follows Graham to town. Rev. Jesse Jackson will speak in the same convention center to the Institute for Democratic Socialists, described by a Jackson spokesman as a "coalition of progressive groups." That minister will receive the full press treatment because he has faith in the kingdoms of this world. He is the kind of preacher the press always likes to follow.

Driving home, I pass the White House. Across the street in Lafayette Park, five people lie on the ground next to a sign that reads, "For World Peace." A television camera records the scene. Just blocks away, where hundreds of people have come forward to say they have found real peace, no one records the event. To viewers of the evening newscasts, it is as if it never happened.

May 4, 1986

FORTY-THREE

NO ROOM IN
THE FRESNO INN

Why is it that virtually every other form of speech and belief is vehemently defended by the self-proclaimed guardians of the First Amendment, except one?

The city attorney of Fresno, California, has ordered the Salvation Army's public service ads removed from city buses after he received complaints from only two people who did not like what the ads said. The ads, which are used in transit systems throughout the nation during November and December to promote the charity's work among the poor, say "Sharing is Caring . . . God bless you." According to Roger McLemore, the Salvation Army's Fresno spokesman, the two people who complained were offended by the ad's reference to God.

McLemore says, "That message certainly is nonsectarian and nondenominational. It's against our grain not to be able to say 'God bless you.' This incenses us."

And well it should.

One can always tell when Christmas is coming, not just by the decorations that begin going up in shopping malls as early as Halloween, but by the number of individuals and organizations who oppose the way some people choose to observe it.

In recent years there have been lawsuits over the display of religious artifacts such as creches and other observances on public property. Other cases include a privately purchased cross on a fire station in Connecticut, a manger scene in a public park in Scarsdale, N.Y., and the Pageant of Peace on the Ellipse behind the White House in Washington.

Never mind that people who observe Christmas for its religious significance are part of the public whose taxes go for the upkeep of public property.

Some holiday detractors argue that any official acknowledgement or observance of Christmas violates the First Amendment. Very well. Let them propose that all government offices remain open on Christmas Day and that all school children be required to attend classes. No politician interested in staying in office would back such a proposal.

Surely, Fresno's censorship of the Salvation Army message proves that intolerance has more than one face.

Three months ago, the city of Baltimore allowed Planned Parenthood to place signs on its public buses that read, "What's an Orgy?" Planned Parenthood said that the ads were intended to promote conversations about sex between children and their parents. Surely, more than two people were offended by that ad, yet the city did not withdraw them.

Why is it that virtually every other form of speech and belief is vehemently defended by the self-proclaimed guardians of the First Amendment, except one?

Would the Fresno City Attorney have yanked an ad on city buses for the movies "Oh God" or "Jesus Christ, Superstar," if church-going residents said it offended them? It seems unlikely.

Why is it that only positive references about God fall outside the protection of the First Amendment? I suspect it is because we live in an age of creeping secularization. The erosion of "free exercise" rights has occurred so slowly and relentlessly that many people are unaware of the threat. It is because those who say they are offended by this sort of thing do nothing about it.

Blacks have learned that eternal vigilance is the price of liberty. So have the Jews. Stereotype a woman in public and feminists loudly complain. When members of these groups sense racism, anti-Semitism, or sexism, pickets often appear, news conferences are held, boycotts are called, consciousness is raised.

What has God done to deserve such a bad reputation that He has become a kind of undesirable alien who is to be banned from the public square? Why is virtually every other thought welcomed as a potential contribution to the country, but God is *persona non grata*?

And why is the Salvation Army under attack in 1986? It has

been publicly God-blessing people since the establishment of its kettle program in San Francisco in 1917.

If the city attorney of Fresno does not reverse himself and allow the Salvation Army ads on public buses, he will have been responsible for adding another dubious distinction to Fresno's recent honors: Godforsaken.

Does the city of Fresno need more grief after qualifying as the "least livable" of 277 urban areas in a State University of New York survey?

November 30, 1986

FORTY - FOUR

TOO MUCH BAGGAGE

*The secular and religious left . . . think it is fine for homosexuals
. . . to be out of the closet, but God is to be kept locked inside and the
door bolted.*

In rejecting Herbert E. Ellingwood to head the office that
screens candidates for federal judgeships, Attorney General
Edwin Meese III is reported to have felt that it would be too
difficult for Ellingwood to win Senate confirmation. Yet, it was
the White House that hung tough on Meese's nomination to
head the Justice Department and fought hard for thirteen
months until he was confirmed. Still, it was felt that Ellingwood,
in the words of one "Senate official," carries "too much baggage."

What is this "baggage" that Ellingwood is said to carry?

Does it match any of Meese's baggage? Is it cronyism? Is it
ill-advised loans and other questionable business deals? It is
none of these. What is thought to have made Ellingwood's confirmation impossible is his religious faith. Ellingwood refuses to
keep his faith in the closet, and that is a no-no except when one
uses faith to promote the kingdom of this world.

Ellingwood believes that "as a man thinketh, so is he." He believes that it is important to determine the philosophy by which a
candidate for the federal bench lives if that philosophy will influence how the judge decides cases.

Certain liberal groups, which had launched a preemptive
strike on Ellingwood's nomination before it was made, believe
that as well, but only when such philosophy lines up with their
political agenda. So Bishop Tutu, Allan Boesak, and Jesse
Jackson, ordained clergyman all, are seen as properly applying
their faith-based world views, but Herb Ellingwood is not.

The secular and religious left would have us believe that to select anyone for the federal bench who takes his or her faith seriously and seeks to apply it to all of life is to act in a way that is not in the interest of the country and that is unconstitutional. Such persons think it is fine for homosexuals, for example, to be out of the closet, but God is to be kept locked inside and the door bolted.

I telephoned two judges with whom I am acquainted to learn their views on faith and works. Both are active Christian laymen.

Federal Judge Woodrow Seals of Houston is an active Methodist. He tells me, "We live in a moral universe and ultimately all our problems — political, economic, and social — should be solved in the moral arena. I'm not a Humanist. I'm a Christian and I look for Christian faith to guide me in moral matters."

Seals tells me he cannot separate his faith from what he does. "My moral code is primarily derived from my Christian faith. If I ever reach the stage where I had to choose between the two, I would resign the bench.

"Everybody has a philosophy of life and philosophy of religion. Mine is Christian. That doesn't mean I'll hold one way because I'm a Christian. There is a fine line that must be drawn." Seals says his faith in God helps him to deal justly with all who come before his court.

"My Christian faith teaches me that each person has great value and is unique because he is a child of God," he says.

Fred Webber is a member of the Montana Supreme Court. He believes that "justice is one of the cardinal points in Scripture in dozens of places. I believe that because of God's interest in justice, there is no contradiction at all between seeking to follow God's standards and the Constitution."

These men don't sound like fanatics to me. Neither does Herb Ellingwood.

There is a new bigotry sweeping America. Every perversion seems to have a support group. Many enjoy the protection of laws that prohibit discrimination against them because of gender, race, or "sexual preference." In Los Angeles, there is a new law on the books to protect AIDS victims from "discrimination." But those who want to take God out of the church building and apply Him in a way that will promote the general welfare,

are told they must not do so because of the so-called "separation of church and state."

In Lynch vs. Donnelly (the 1984 Nativity Scene case), the Supreme Court said that a "total separation of (church and state) is not possible." It further stated that the word "wall" that is supposed to divide the two is only a "metaphor" and that "no significant segment of our society and no institution within it can exist in a vacuum or in total or absolute isolation from all other parts, much less from government."

And yet, a vacuum is precisely what some of those who opposed Herb Ellingwood's nomination are seeking to create.

Law originated in the Old Testament. In the New Testament are highlighted such concepts as mercy and pardon. To pretend that the law is simply the idea of men is to engage in a serious form of plagiarism.

In selectively proof-texting the Founding Fathers, liberals frequently overlook such statements as this one by James Madison, who helped write the Bill of Rights: "We have staked the whole future of American civilization, not upon the power of government, far from it. We have staked the future of all of our political institutions upon the capacity of mankind for self-government; upon the capacity of each and all of us to govern ourselves, to control ourselves, to sustain ourselves according to the Ten Commandments of God."

It is a good thing Mr. Madison is not around today. The ACLU would say he is unfit to be President and that his remarks violate the Constitution.

September 5, 1985

FORTY-FIVE

THE OTHER SIDE OF INTOLERANCE

Christopher Sundseth was fired for having in his thought world a belief in something more powerful than the state. That is a heresy that must be quickly punished by the secular mind lest the idea catch on.

There are very few things that can get you fired from a government job these days. Making ethnic and gender jokes can. Sexual harassment can. But even certain forms of stealing do not automatically result in termination, so long as the thefts are not too large and "everyone else is doing it."

Nowadays it seems the grounds for dismissal from a government job (and a ground for not hiring you in the first place) include expressing your religious beliefs.

Christopher C. Sundseth, a Treasury Department economist detailed to the Inter-American Development Bank, found this out the hard way. When a California man contended in a letter to an Education Department employee that the United States was never "a Christian nation," Sundseth wrote back, "This country was founded by Christians who were escaping the same kind of small-minded tripe you espouse."

Representative Patricia Schroeder (D-Colorado) called Sundseth's response "insulting and derogatory" and demanded that he be fired. He was — though a Treasury Department official says he would have been let go anyway. But isn't that what they always say?

Sundseth could see the handwriting on the wall when he was not invited to the signing by Treasury Secretary James A. Baker of a new agreement involving the United States and thirty-four other nations that make up the Inter-American Investment Corporation. It was a project Sundseth had been working on since February of last year. Office secretaries were invited to the ceremony. His was the only name on a list of 260 persons that was scratched following adverse publicity about this letter.

The point is not whether Sundseth was tactful in his letter, or even whether some might judge him guilty of saying the wrong thing. What if Sundseth were an atheist and the letter writer had said this IS a "Christian nation"? What if atheist Sundseth had responded that the writer was a fool for believing in religion? Would Sundseth have been fired? No way, because religious discrimination is a one-way street.

If Sundseth had favored a policy that would require this country to be called a "Christian nation" and penalize people who believe otherwise, that would have been an entirely different matter. But he advocated no such thing, and his freedom-of-speech rights under the First Amendment should have afforded him protection to say what he thinks.

Earlier this year, Herbert Ellingwood was denied a Justice Department job that involved screening of federal judge candidates because he is an active Christian layman and used to lead Bible studies at the White House.

Had either of these men been followers of, say, the Baghwan Rajneesh, their beliefs and behavior might have been viewed as quaint, but the alarm would not have been sounded at civil liberties headquarters.

If Sundseth had worn a dress and donned a pig's snout to jump up and down as a "hogette" at Washington Redskins football games he would have done nothing deserving of opposition. In fact, he could count on support from his fellow "fans." But because Sundseth believes in God between Sundays, he is not a fan, but a "fanatic" in the minds of those who do not share similar beliefs.

The late philosopher-theologian Dr. Francis Schaeffer observed, "There is a flow to history and culture. This flow is rooted and has its wellspring in the thoughts of people. People are unique in the inner life of the mind — what they are in their thought world determines how they act. This is true of their value systems and it is true of their creativity. It is true of their corporate actions such as political decisions, and it is true of their personal lives. The results of their thought world flow through their fingers or from their tongues into the external world."

Christopher Sundseth was fired for having in his thought world a belief in something more powerful than the state. That is a heresy which must be quickly punished by the secular mind lest the idea catch on. Should that happen, people like Congresswoman Schroeder and her fellow "gurus," whose thought worlds begin at a different source, might find themselves looking for work.

November 24, 1985

FORTY - SIX

TAXATION WITHOUT REPRESENTATION

. . . Parents are forced to subsidize a line of thinking that is the antithesis of what they believe and what they teach their children at church and at home.

One of the rallying cries that fueled the American Revolution was opposition to "taxation without representation." The colonists were not about to pay taxes to a government in which they had no voice.

Taxation without representation is precisely what the textbook battle in Greenville, Tennessee, was all about. Conservative taxpaying Christian parents won an important court case recently when they persuaded a federal judge that required reading materials went against their religious beliefs. U.S. District Court Judge Thomas G. Hull said children of those parents may opt out of reading assignments that contradicted their beliefs, and instead may be taught at home with materials acceptable to their parents.

When I was in high school, prior to becoming an English literature major in college, I was required to read some of the works that drew objections from the Greenville parents. I, however, was not morally or intellectually immobilized or secularized. Instead I became a conservative!

The difference was that during my school days in the 1950s and early '60s the American culture more reflected the values of the plaintiffs in the Tennessee textbook case than it does today. Students could be taught to think critically because they were presented with different views, and religiously based values were usually a part of that presentation.

Not so today. As one of the plaintiff parents observed, "There's not one story in all the readers . . . that supports or portrays the traditional family role. . . . The few times Christianity was presented in the readers, it was always negative."

Had the parents been black and complained about the exclusion of positive black role models for their children, there would have been no outcry from the educational establishment. In fact, there were complaints from black parents a few years ago over assigned readings of "Little Black Sambo" in some public schools. Those legitimate objections led to the book's being dropped from required reading lists.

Had the plaintiffs been of the feminist persuasion and objected that the required readings presented a distorted or unfair view of women, the education establishment would have gone along. In fact, feminist guidelines for textbook writing continue to be used by the major publishing houses.

More recently, homosexual rights advocates have also found sympathetic ears at textbook publishing houses.

Only when the religiously committed person raises a protest that his views are not represented in obligatory reading is he told, "If you don't like what is taught here, start your own schools." One network reporter summed up the attitude of some Greenville parents in just about those words. Anyone who dared to suggest alternative schools for blacks or feminists who didn't like the textbooks would be fried in the deep fat of boiling editorial pages and public opinion.

Perhaps some parents might agree to educate their children privately if the government would give them back the money they pay in taxes for the public schools. But instead parents are forced to subsidize a line of thinking that is the antithesis of what they believe and what they teach their children at church and at home.

Some argue that the court ruling will inhibit the plaintiff children's ability to think critically. But the parents argue, correctly in my view, that it is the absence of religiously based values that inhibits critical thinking, because that absence forces children to accept a one-dimensional view of life. Failing to understand religion and its power in motivating men and women for good and for ill is to ignore a characteristic of humanity, a power pollster George Gallup has said is a greater motivator of behavior than gender, race, economic conditions, or educational background.

The Tennessee case was not really a trial about excellence in education or the lack thereof. It was about who will mold and control the minds of the next generation during their formative years.

The "opt out" approach is not the best answer over the long term because it opens the door for others to challenge the curricula based on various personal beliefs. A better solution would be to provide an all-inclusive education program that exposes students to a variety of values and beliefs. That was the kind of program we used to have in the days of the *McGuffey Readers*, and children turned out well educated and well rounded then.

The Tennessee trial was dubbed "Scopes II" because it was said to replay the 1925 evolution vs. creation trial. That trial resulted in public opinion eventually turning in favor of those who believe humans descended from monkeys. If this was a replay, then the monkeys lost this time around.

October 30, 1986

FORTY-SEVEN

A CONSPIRACY
OF SILENCE

*. . . The greatest civil rights, medical, moral, and intellectual issue
of our time has been largely ignored by the press, which makes a habit of
shoving its collective nose into everything else.*

Think about the events and anniversaries of events that are
observed each January. And think of what they all have in
common.

Each January marks the anniversary of the return of the
American hostages from Iran and the inauguration of the Presi-
dent. January is also the birth month of Martin Luther King,
Jr., for which we now have a national holiday.

Then there are events that at first glance do not seem to be
peculiar to January, but that have attracted the attention of the
public each January (largely because they have attracted the
attention of the media each January). These include the plight of
the "homeless," who are about to be immortalized in a January
made-for-TV film, and of the victims of the disease AIDS, which
NBC News spent yet another hour discussing in a January
prime-time special. And let us not forget the Ethiopian famine.
We are the world, remember?

What all of these subjects have in common aside from their
January emphasis is the sweeping attention the press has heaped
upon them. And yet the greatest civil rights, medical, moral,
and intellectual issue of our time has been largely ignored by the
press, which makes a habit of shoving its collective nose into
everything else.

January 22 marks the anniversary of the Supreme Court's
Roe vs. Wade decision, which struck down the life-protecting

laws of fifty states without a debate and with no national consensus that what the court did was correct. Unlike the above-mentioned events and subjects, the press and particularly television, from which we get the majority of our news and views, has engaged in what I would call a "conspiracy of silence" on the subject.

I am not given to conspiracy theories, and I do not suggest that this has been the result of meetings at which it was agreed not to cover abortion with anything approaching the depth reserved for issues such as AIDS. It is, instead, a decision to treat abortion not as a subject steeped in morality, as the Vietnam war became, but as just another exercise in power politics, with the "prize" going to the side that turns out the most votes or demonstrators. This view is rooted in the philosophy advanced by the late Supreme Court Justice Charles Evans Hughes, who observed that "the Constitution is what the judges say it is."

Television has a public responsibility, indeed a national duty consistent with the freedoms it has been given (and which it so often asserts for itself), to provide the nation with the facts about abortion. Television has an obligation to show pictures, as it did during the civil rights marches and the war in Vietnam (and continues to do when reminding us of another holocaust in Nazi Germany). These pictures helped us make up our collective minds about policies we were to pursue. Without the pictures, the policies might have been different. We have truth-in-lending and truth-in-packaging laws. What about "truth in utero"?

Whatever else might be involved in the debate over human life, it is decidedly not just a question of which side has the most votes. To suggest that this is all the debate is about is to accept Stalin's cynical remark when told of the Pope's criticism of him: "How many divisions does the Pope have?"

In recent days I have spoken with two Florida women who have had abortions. One, Suzanne Towne, said she was ignorant about abortion, but decided to have one because she was unmarried and a "counselor" told her that her baby was "nothing but a piece of tissue." The second woman, Kay Hammer, said her doctor told her he recommended an abortion because she had been taking large doses of a tranquilizer and he could not be sure how the baby might be affected.

Both women said if they had known more they would not have gone through with the procedure. Both women said they have suffered severe depression and guilt and now know what they did was "murder" (their word) their babies.

In an age when nothing is sacred and every subject is fit for examination by the omnivorous media, why this conspiracy of silence on abortion? Why can we see close-up pictures of a mobster gunned down in the streets of New York or pictures of the slaughtered passengers (complete with pools of blood and contorted faces) at the airports in Rome and Vienna, but nothing of this sort on abortion?

To be sure, there was the 1984 film, "The Silent Scream," but the television networks spent more time interviewing "experts" who said the film was a fraud than they did exploring the subject of abortion and what really happens to the baby and to the woman during the procedure. Neither have they followed up women who have had abortions and spoken with them about the physical, emotional, and spiritual complications of the operation.

The late Bishop Fulton Sheen (I am reluctant to mention the name of a prominent Catholic here for fear of raising the bigotry that abortion is just a "Catholic issue") once observed that "there is no freedom given without an accompanying responsibility."

The television networks have been granted virtually unlimited freedom regarding the content of their programs. When they pay attention to abortion in their entertainment programming, such as recent episodes of "Cagney and Lacey" and "St. Elsewhere," it is usually to indulge in stereotype. It is long past the time when the networks ought to have been demonstrating some responsibility and begun fueling, through pictures and rational discussion, the national debate on abortion that the country has lacked for a decade and a half. It is a debate we all desperately need to see take place.

January 26, 1986

FORTY-EIGHT

THE RELIGION OF HUMANISM

It is hypocritical to say that a view you support must not be censored and that one you oppose must be excluded, but hypocrisy has always been one of the liberal's strongest suits.

Last summer, "civil liberties" groups were crowing over their victory in the Alabama school prayer case. The Supreme Court, by a vote of 6-to-3, struck down a state law that permitted a daily minute of silent meditation or prayer in the Alabama public schools.

But now, adopting a strategy often used by their opponents, a group of six hundred Mobile County parents has returned to court claiming that their religious views are discriminated against by the exclusive teaching of humanism in the same schools in which it is considered unconstitutional to meditate or pray silently.

This time the parents have an important ally in Governor George C. Wallace, who has agreed with the Supreme Court that "humanism is a religion" and that it is advanced in some public school textbooks in violation of the First Amendment. In effect, the parents are saying that if mentioning God is a violation of the Constitution, ignoring the impact of those who have believed in Him is, too.

The governor's declaration of humanism as a religion comes in the midst of a complex court suit brought by religious conservatives who say they want "the religion of humanism" removed from Alabama public schools.

Chief U.S. District Judge Brevard Hand, who will hear the

143

case, already is on record as believing that humanism is a religion and that it is being promoted in the textbooks.

In the Alabama prayer case, Judge Hand observed, "The religions of atheism, materialism, agnosticism, communism, and socialism have escaped the scrutiny of the courts throughout the years, and make no mistake these are to the believers religions; they are ardently adhered to and quantitatively advanced in the teachings and literature that is presented to the fertile minds of the students in the various school systems. . . . An example of what the Court heard reflecting on this point is in connection with the claimed use of foul language in literature read by a fourth grader and, though it might seem innocuous to some to condemn the use of the word 'Goddamn' as it is used in the writings that are required reading, it can clearly be argued that as to Christianity it is blasphemy and is the establishment of an advancement of humanism, secularism, or agnosticism. If the state cannot teach or advance Christianity, how can it teach or advance the Antichrist?"

If you do not think this is an example of discrimination, find a book in which you read "Mosesdamn" or "Buddhadamn" or "Moondamn." Using the name of God alone clearly discriminates against those to whom God is more than a prefix to a curse word.

Commenting on the deliberate exclusion of religious history and contributions to America in a recent *Wall Street Journal* article, New York University Professor Paul C. Vitz wrote of his study of sixty representative social studies textbooks: "None of the books covering grades one through four contained one word referring to any religious activity in contemporary American life . . . not one word referred to any child or adult who prayed, or who went to church or temple. A few rare pictures (without captions) did depict Jewish or Catholic religious scenes, but not one word or image in these books showed any form of contemporary Protestantism."

Imagine if this was the case with women or blacks, two groups whose protestations have been heard and who are now widely included along with historical and contemporary role models for students to study. And yet, even though more people attend religious services on a given weekend than attend all professional sports contests combined, religion is virtually excluded from the textbooks.

William A. Jackson, a legal adviser to Governor Wallace, signed a document on behalf of the governor in which he stipulated that Christianity and its role in American society have been censored from textbooks used in Alabama schools. Jackson said, "The governor of Alabama agrees that such demonstrated censorship of the existence, history, contributions, and roles of Protestantism, Catholicism, and Judaism constitutes unconstitutional discrimination against religion in violation of the First Amendment."

It is an interesting approach and may be the first time that contemporary humanism — the belief that God does not exist and the belief in the scientific and philosophical teachings that flow from such a presupposition — has been regarded as an article of religious faith and, therefore, unfit for presentation to those "impressionable minds" who supposedly are injured by exposure to the possibility of the existence of God.

Lawyers for the American Civil Liberties Union and People for the American Way argued the prayer case based on church-state separation. This time they will argue the case based on censorship. It is hypocritical to say that a view you support must not be censored and that one you oppose must be excluded, but hypocrisy has always been one of the liberal's strongest suits.

February 13, 1986

FORTY-NINE

THERE'S MORE THAN ONE WAY TO CENSOR

It is one thing to debate whether books and ideas should be pulled out of schools and off library shelves. It is at least as dangerous to keep selected ideas from seeing the light of day.

A dangerous and far more subtle form of censorship than that practiced by publicity-hungry book-banners is taking place in this country. It is the prevention of the publication of certain ideas because some employees of the publishing houses consider these ideas anathema.

George Gilder, whose phenomenally successful book *Wealth and Poverty* became the economics manifesto of the Reagan Administration when it was published inn 1980, is the author of an earlier book called *Sexual Suicide*. The 1973 work argues that marriage and the family give direction to men's lives and channel their inherent aggressiveness into providing for their families. Gilder believes that the sexual revolution and the breakdown of sex roles are destroying the family structure, which in turn is leading to economic disparity and to husbands abandoning their wives for younger women.

Is this an idea worthy of continuing debate in print? The bigtime New York publishing houses don't think so. According to Gilder, publishers defend their refusal to publish an updated version of *Sexual Suicide* under the title *Men and Marriage* on the grounds that feminists on their staffs don't like Gilder's ideas.

In an interview, Gilder said, ". . . the sociology of New York publishing has created a brick wall for this type of book. There are at many houses a body of editors who are committed to feminism and just don't like books that don't support feminist arguments."

Carol Felsenthal, a feminist writer, has a complaint about the way her well-balanced biography of anti-ERA leader Phyllis Schlafly was handled by booksellers. Felsenthal said that feminists harassed salespersons from Doubleday and Company who tried to promote *The Sweetheart of the Silent Majority,* and that "in some cities major book chains refused to carry the book."

"When they do handle it," Felsenthal said, "it's almost certain to be buried on some bottom shelf. There are lots of ways to kill a book and most of them have been used on *Sweetheart.*"

Another censorship twist involves the publication of the "Final Report of the Attorney General on Pornography." Some in the publishing and book-selling industries who have railed against the findings, which they consider to be attempts at censorship, seem to be quietly but effectively censoring the report. Despite the fact that the first printing of fifty thousand copies sold out in a little over a month through largely private channels, Waldenbooks has ordered only 250 copies, or about one book for every four stores, and B. Dalton has ordered only five hundred, or close to one book per store. Zondervan, the sixth largest chain and the biggest Christian publisher, is refusing to carry it at all, apparently because of the sexually explicit content.

Though these incidents of censorship do not receive much publicity, they are serious ones that watchdogs ought to address. It is one thing to debate whether books and ideas should be pulled out of schools and off library shelves. It is at least as dangerous to keep selected ideas from seeing the light of day.

November 11, 1986

PART FOUR

DOMESTIC
DISPUTE

FIFTY

WHAT IS A FAMILY?

. . . There is a connection between strong families and the state of the Union . . .

The *New York Times* recently printed an ad showing a woman wearing a sad expression and a fox coat. The headline read, "The 'divorce is final' coat." The ad copy read, "O.K., so it didn't work out. The important thing to remember is that there are lots of other people out there who have gone through the very same thing. And also remember that there are lots of people out there to fall in love with again. Well . . . maybe not LOTS. But certainly one or two. Shed the tears and slip into a fur. . . . So you lost the man of your dreams. Find the fur of your dreams."

While unintentionally so, this is a sad commentary on the state of family life and the decline in underlying values. The husband has been shed and in his place is a new coat, an ultimate symbol of materialism. Why worry? the ad asks. It has happened to lots of others.

Indeed it has. It is, however, something we should be worried about.

The recently released Report of the Working Group on the Family to the White House Domestic Policy Council makes that very clear.

The heart of the issue is contained in this paragraph from the report: "The idols of our recent past were those who defied norms and shattered standards, and indeed there is always a place for 'rebels.' But in a healthy society, heroes are the women and men who hold the world together one home at a time: the parents and grandparents who forgo pleasures, delay purchases, foreclose options, and commit most of their lives to the noblest undertaking of citizenship: raising children who, resting on the shoulders of the previous generation, will see farther than we and reach higher."

This is no crusade for moralism masquerading as public policy. The report says there is a connection between strong families and the state of the Union: "The breakdown of the American family in recent years merely confirms the interdependence of strong families and secure liberties. Irresponsibility, self-seeking, and contempt of authority erode not only the family but respect for law and civility as well. Children who do not learn to live out commitments to others in a family do not learn to live within a larger society either. If we wish to see a renewal of liberty, we must work for a renaissance of the family."

Critics of the report were quick to remind us that it deals not with contemporary reality, but with a time and a view of the family as it used to be. This may be true, but there are larger questions: Are we happy with the way things have turned out after twenty years of no-fault divorce, open marriages, and other social experiments? If not, is it possible to reclaim some of those old values for a more secure and better future?

At the recent Catholic Bishops meeting in Washington, there was a call for a greater government role in binding up the nation's wounds, which have been inflicted, at least partly, by the destruction of families. But we have twenty years of history that prove that government spending and government social programs are not the best answers.

We have erroneously come to believe that we can destroy foundations and the lovely buildings will not topple. As C. S. Lewis wrote in 1943, "We remove the organ and demand the function. We make men without chests and expect of them virtue and enterprise. We laugh at honor and are shocked to find traitors in our midst." Though describing his era, Lewis was a prophet for our time.

In speaking of true compassion to help the needy, who are often the victims of family breakdown, the Working Group report says, "We now need to agree that such help to be really compassionate must not rob the needy of the motivations, aspirations, family loyalties, values, and character traits that ultimately are the only engine that drives families out of poverty and dependency to self-sufficiency."

Knowing the difference between the misspent "compassion" born of bureaucratic government and that born of true commitment, either within the family or on the part of those who would truly help, is the first step in countering the forces that have led to the decline of family values.

November 23, 1986

FIFTY - ONE

WHAT HATH *NOW* WROUGHT?

Has NOW, which was formed from the ashes of burning brassieres, succeeded in liberating women? It depends on your definition of "succeed."

The National Organization for Women held a twentieth anniversary party for itself last week. The press, as usual, covered it with the uncritical eye it reserves for trendy movements. Television news would have us believe that nearly all women are feminists and the few who are not are an irrelevant subgroup hardly worthy of notice.

Has NOW, which was formed from the ashes of burning brassieres, succeeded in liberating women? It depends on your definition of "succeed." The dictionary says the word means "to turn out well." Have things turned out well for women as a result of NOW's feminist agenda? For many, I believe, they have not.

Marabel Morgan, author of *Total Joy* and other books that infuriate feminists because of their emphasis on the home as a woman's primary source of fulfillment, says, "The desire for satisfaction and success is universal, but millions of women have discovered that [while] getting married and having children does not completely fulfill [them], a nine-to-five job doesn't produce peace. Prestige and power do not bring happiness. Money and education do not produce a happy atmosphere at the breakfast table." Morgan believes a woman who is not at peace within herself will never find happiness in externals such as a career.

It was Lenin who taught that a revolutionary need not be concerned with what follows the tearing down of societal structures. A revolutionary's job is simply to tear them down and leave it to others to build something in their place.

The feminist revolution spawned by NOW against the home as a primary societal foundation and the source of fulfillment for women and men has "succeeded" in that it has torn the home apart. A majority of men are uncomfortable with the role of "Mr. Mom," or a spouse who is as tired as they are after a long day's work, and having kids stashed in the day-care center. Increasing numbers of women, too, are saying they feel uncomfortable with the double life. When having the opportunity to choose between career and rearing children, at least in their early years, more women are opting for the kids.

The fact is, while many women have liberated themselves from a primary family role, so, too, have many men. The glue that once bound men to their mates has been dissolving rapidly and increasing numbers of women are now fending for themselves. The results are that in the first year after divorce, the standard of living for men rises 42 percent while that of women drops 72 percent, according to a Stanford University study. No-fault divorce laws, which since 1970 have been adopted by every state except South Dakota, have brought incredible hardship to divorced women and their children. Is this the price of liberation?

The figures show that the cultural instability created by the breakup of families is clearly a national problem, and a special one for women.

Lyndon Johnson once said, "Unless we work to strengthen the family, to create conditions under which most parents will stay together—all the rest: schools and playgrounds, and public assistance, and private concern will never be enough to cut completely the circle of despair and deprivation."

Twenty years of NOW is enough. After seeing what NOW has wrought, one wishes there had been a choice between NOW or never.

December 7, 1986

FIFTY-TWO

PORNOGRAPHY WARS

There are currently more stores selling pornographic videos than there are McDonald hamburger stands.

What would you think of a government commission that was unable to cast a majority vote in favor of this proposition: "The family is the basic societal unit of society, and therefore, the health and vitality of an entire nation is dependent upon the integrity of that individual family structure"?

When asked to vote on this proposition at a meeting of the Attorney General's Commission on Pornography, members deadlocked 5-to-5.

"It's a mess," says one knowledgeable source close to the commission about the prospects of its coming to grips with what increasing numbers of people view as pornography's growing threat to the social stability created by the family.

There is no debate among the commissioners about the harmfulness of two categories of pornography: that which is "vulgar, degrading, humiliating, and subjugating, including sado-masochism; and that which is all of the above, but non-violent."

What divides the commissioners and threatens to produce a stillborn report is a third category: consensual, non-violent, non-humiliating pornography. Examples would be promiscuity, adultery, adult incest, and explicit sexual activity between more than one man and/or more than one woman.

Most people, even most pornographers, agree that youngsters deserve to be shielded from pornographic materials. But a recent study by Canadian professor James B. Check at the University of York in Ontario discovered that young people are consuming pornography in numbers greater than ever before.

The Check study found that youth between twelve and seventeen had the highest interest in pornographic materials and were its prime purchasers.

Another study was conducted of one hundred males and one hundred females in each of three age categories: junior high, high school, and adult nineteen to thirty-nine. It found that 91 percent of males and 82 percent of females had seen a magazine that depicted couples or groups engaged in explicit sexual acts; the average age for first viewing such materials was thirteen-and-a-half; a larger percentage of high school students had seen X-rated films than any other age group, including adults; 46 percent of junior high students had seen one or more X-rated movies; and the average age for first seeing such a film for these students was fourteen years and eight months.

At a time when the courts and the so-called "civil libertarians" seem concerned about what effects exposure to God might have on "impressionable minds," where is their concern for what effects exposure to pornography might have (and is having) on the same minds?

One commission member believes that pornography is a threat to the future of the family. This member notes that "we are sexual creatures, and the physical attraction between males and females provides the basis for every dimension of marriage and parenthood. Thus, anything that interjects itself into that relationship must be embraced with great caution."

This member believes that if the commission does not determine that forms of pornography that fall into the third category are harmful, then attempts to control its spread will have been dealt a mortal blow.

There are currently more stores selling pornographic videos than there are McDonald hamburger stands, and it is difficult to find a PG movie these days that does not depict some of the behavior that concerns at least half of the commission members.

Is our government really concerned? The Justice Department has come in for some criticism from those who feel that the commission's $500,000 budget is too small (the 1970 presidential commission on pornography received $2 million). Further, critics say, this commission has not been given adequate time to complete its work. They charge the Justice Department has not supported the work of the commission, because many at Justice do not feel that pornography is an important issue. Attorney General Edwin Meese is said by some sources to be far removed from the workings of the commission.

Evidence is mounting that there is at least a connection between pornography and the general decline of a nation's moral water table. Investigations have indicated that people who commit sex crimes are heavy consumers of pornographic materials. And one would have to be a fool to believe that the pervasiveness of sex as a marketable commodity does not contribute to teen pregnancy, venereal disease, and family breakups in the same way that cigarette smoking contributes to cancer and heart disease.

One commission member refers to the pornography problem as "a river of smut." It is time the government took an interest in cleaning up this river for the sake of our children and the shoring up of the already-threatened stability of the American family.

The Attorney General's pornography commission can begin the process by concluding that while pornography might give some people their "jollies," its spread can do irreparable harm to a nation.

April 13, 1986

FIFTY - THREE

WOMEN'S HISTORY WEEK

Know how to tell when feminism is really dead? When Phil Donahue does an entire program on homemaking and none of the women are lesbians.

Some of my colleagues have recently declared feminism to be dead. But, like these premature reports of Mark Twain's demise, feminism has not expired. It has merely retreated behind the protective walls of academia.

Not long ago Women's History Week was celebrated in our land and the only reason I forgot to observe it was because I have come to rely on Merlin Olson to keep me informed of these sorts of things so I can send "tickler bouquets." Merlin must have missed it, too.

When I saw that Trenton State College was in charge of New Jersey's observance of Women's History Week and that actress Meryl Streep, author Judy Blume, and ten other women were being honored for their work in academia, labor, business, government, the military, and the arts, I called the school to find out the names and accomplishments of the other honorees.

They turned out to be professionals, too.

I asked the college public relations director, Jill Anheiser, if there was not one category that was missing?

"Which one?" she asked.

"Homemaker," I said.

After a pause, Ms. Anheiser said, somewhat surprised, "That's true!" She then proceeded to explain that some of the women being honored were at one time homemakers.

"Yes, but no woman is being honored for her success as a

homemaker," I replied. Ms. Anheiser acknowledged that I had a point. This is, after all, the age of "Mr. Mom."

Thinking that the observance of Women's History Week at Trenton State College may have been an aberration, I called the University of Michigan, another school that was observing Women's History Week on behalf of the state.

The public information person at U of M is Ginny Lagather, who informed me, "I was a feminist as soon as I found out I was a girl." She added, "I was born a victim because I was born female."

A planning committee that included Ms. Lagather selected as the two main speakers for Women's History Week at the University of Michigan self-proclaimed Communist Angela Davis and National Organization for Women President Eleanor Smeal. Other speakers also chose to discuss topics that would generally be considered feminist. The "folklorist" who spoke on "The History of Irish Faeries" may have been an exception.

Ms. Lagather tells me, "We selected a variety of people to bring in fresh ideas, not to tell students the things they've heard many times before." By which I suppose she means things such as the joys of running a successful home.

Incredibly, the local Girl Scouts chapter was to be a co-sponsor (along with the YWCA) of the Angela Davis appearance, but it withdrew after a rash of negative publicity. The local Girl Scout chapter is headed by a former board member of Planned Parenthood, who later served on a panel that wrote sex education materials for the public schools.

Ms. Lagather asserts that the political viewpoint of Angela Davis "has nothing to do with why she was brought in." She says (presumably with a straight face, but it is hard to tell over the phone), "It's what she has to say about women that is the reason she was invited. A university, by definition, is a place where a diversity of ideas are to be aired and heard." But not ideas about women as homemakers, it appears.

Beverly LaHaye, who heads the conservative 560,000-member Concerned Women of America, senses a resistance to this propagandizing by feminists on college campuses.

"Eight years ago," says Mrs. LaHaye, "college women would not listen to people like me. Now, I am receiving invitations from schools such as the University of Texas and Georgetown

University to speak about traditional values and lifestyles. There is more interest in the value of being a wife, a mother, and a homemaker."

School textbooks, vocational guidance materials, and most women's magazines also ignore homemaking as an honorable profession. But, according to Phyllis Schlafly, there are at least fourteen million single-earner couples and millions more with the spouse working only part time. And the numbers appear to be growing as more women conclude that a career alone cannot make them happy or fulfilled. Who knows how many women would prefer to stay at home, but cannot because of economic necessity?

Now, how to tell when feminism is really dead? When Phil Donahue does an entire program on homemaking and none of the women are lesbians.

March 13, 1986

THE CRISIS IN BLACK AMERICA

. . . It was the civil libertarians who helped get black Americans into this fix, . . . emphasizing freedom without responsibility.

When it comes to blaming America first, those "San Francisco Democrats," of whom Jeane Kirkpatrick spoke at the 1984 Republican National Convention, have nothing on those black political leaders who blame Ronald Reagan first for everything bad that happens to black people.

In a "State of Black America" report, the National Urban League blamed much of the economic disparity between black and white Americans on the President, who, it said, has acted as a "Rambo-like destroyer of civil rights gains."

A more precise examination of the real reason for the crisis in black America was conducted by CBS News. Correspondent Bill Moyers spent half of a "CBS Reports" special interviewing young blacks (the third generation of those without fathers, living with mothers on welfare) and the rest of the program talking with four black leaders. Moyers was the only white on the program, which was good because it forced the participants to focus on the issue at hand and avoid political debates and recriminations. This was a family matter and no "outsiders" were needed.

The program was one of the best documentaries ever put on television. Moyers, though a political liberal, resisted all of the temptations that could have earned him brownie points with his friends and got right to the heart of the matter.

The reason why 60 percent of all black children are born out of wedlock and why half of all black teenage girls become pregnant, and the reason for the "sexual recklessness" among black teens has nothing to do with Ronald Reagan. It has to do instead with a breakdown in the black family unprecedented in this or perhaps any other culture.

What was so remarkable about this program was the transparency of all the participants. There was no Reagan-bashing, not even by Jesse Jackson. In fact, it was Jackson who said that what is needed to remedy the crisis in black America is a "massive counter-cultural movement" by those who have the ears of the young people. Jackson noted that by the time a child is fifteen, he or she has been exposed to eighteen thousand hours of television, which has included seven hundred thousand murders; twenty thousand hours of radio; less than eleven thousand hours of school and less than three thousand hours of church. So the mass media, which is constantly spewing forth its message of hedonism, has a greater impact than home, church, and school combined.

Said Jackson, "Someone must say that babies making babies and kids taking drugs is morally wrong."

Newark police detective Shahib Jackson called for more self-control and self-esteem. He observed that "Freedom is a lot of times destruction; the more freedom a man has, a lot of times he'll just self-destruct. Somebody has to say, 'No, you can't do this.'"

Howard University psychologist Dr. George Jackson said that the nation has lost its foundations.

Others on the program spoke of a return to "traditional values," of a need for "moral regeneration" to reverse "moral degeneracy," of the "outrageous music" that many blacks listen to, which is loaded with sexual overtones, and of the lack of "absolute morality."

If I had not seen this program with my own eyes and heard it with my own years, I might have thought it had been produced by a group of right-wing fundamentalist preachers and politicians. Yet, here were the best and the brightest of liberaldom, writing the same prescription.

One participant said what is needed is a "drumbeat" that will tell young blacks the right way from the wrong way. And, she said, it will need to come from every quarter, not just from the black community.

Only once during the broadcast special was the question of civil liberties raised and whether it would be constitutionally permissible to place metal detectors inside schools to discover guns and knives brought in by students. The raising of such a question is an indication of why we have the problems we have.

The preamble to the Constitution speaks of promoting the GENERAL welfare, not everyone's welfare. The welfare of no one is promoted by black teenage pregnancies, by drugs, by welfare of a different sort, and by a breakdown in the black family. Besides, it was the civil libertarians who helped get black Americans into this fix in the first place, emphasizing freedom without responsibility.

Surely white and black conservatives can join with their more liberal white and black countrymen to help restore the foundations in the black community. Without that restoration, in the words of Dr. George Jackson of Howard University, "It won't be long before others in the population are affected."

The fact is, they already are.

January 30, 1986

FIFTY - FIVE

WOMAN POWER

As if political defeat were not bad enough, what the feminists thought was their natural constituency, career-minded women, are beginning to desert the ranks and seek fulfillment as mothers and homemakers.

"I am woman, hear me roar, in numbers too big to ignore. . . ." So went the Helen Reddy song of the last decade. It was supposed to be the national anthem of the feminist movement that would usher in a new political force to be reckoned with. But did it?

While much of the press has conferred celebrity status on women with names such as Betty Friedan, Eleanor Smeal, and Judy Goldsmith, the real political impact is coming from women with such names as Candy Lightner, Joyce Nalepka, Beverly LaHaye, Jeane Kirkpatrick, Kandy Stroud, and Phyllis Schlafly.

Candy Lightner founded Mothers Against Drunk Drivers (MADD) after her daughter was killed by a drunk. The group has succeeded in strengthening drunk driving laws and persuading state legislatures to raise the drinking age for all alcoholic beverages.

Joyce Nalepka founded Parents for a Drug Free Youth, which was successful in getting legislation passed that outlawed "head shops," stores that sell drug paraphernalia.

Kandy Stroud, along with a group of women married to members of Congress, has successfully lobbied the recording industry to place advisories on their albums and cassettes, warning of sexually explicit material.

Beverly LaHaye is president of the Concerned Women for America, a rather new conservative lobbying group that has more than doubled its membership to 431,000, compared to the National Organization for Women's paltry 250,000.

Jeane Kirkpatrick's contributions to the nation are surely not over. Already she has redefined the role of United States Ambassador to the United Nations and her voice will continue to be heard in a soon-to-be-syndicated newspaper column, and probably in the 1988 presidential race.

And then there is Phyllis Schlafly, who drives feminists up the wall because of her scholastic and homemaking achievements. Schlafly's Eagle Forum has successfully lobbied, against seemingly impossible odds, to torpedo the Equal Rights Amendment, scuttle the Carter Administration's attempt to draft women for military service, and maintain Social Security benefits for the homemaker. Her group was also instrumental in the passage of the Child Protection Act, which bans child pornography. Schlafly is now involved in a campaign to raise the personal exemption for children, as well as backing the Strategic Defense Initiative (SDI).

And what have the feminists done? They have made a lot of noise and attracted a lot of attention from the press. Other than that, they have given new meaning to the word "shrill." Eleanor Smeal told the tiny NOW convention in New Orleans last month, "People are tired of being told the country has become right wing. They want to fight back." A majority in Minnesota and the District of Columbia, maybe, but in case you missed the last election, Ms. Smeal, Ronald Reagan won forty-nine states in the biggest landslide in history.

As if political defeat were not bad enough, what the feminists thought was their natural constituency, career-minded women, are beginning to desert the ranks and seek fulfillment as mothers and homemakers.

Even the *New York Times*, as staunch a defender of the feminist agenda as exists anywhere, has run more than one article on mothers who are shifting back from jobs to homemaking.

The liberal *Washington Monthly* magazine carried an article as long ago as January, 1982, which was a preview of coming attractions. It was called, "Why Mothers Should Stay Home." The author was Deborah Fallows, who was described as a person who "left her full-time job in linguistics when her second son was born." I wouldn't send her a NOW membership application form, Ellie. She may be too busy rearing the next generation to attend one of your conventions.

So, when the history of this era is written, there will be a fair amount of space given to the Smeals, the Friedans, and the Goldsmiths. But the space given those who were really effective in bringing about meaningful change, resulting in a stronger and better America, will go to women, many of them conservative, who gave something back to their country instead of demanding more for themselves.

August 18, 1985

FIFTY-SIX

"M" IS FOR THE MONEY THAT YOU BRING HOME

. . . A child's future intellectual capacity and emotional security are largely dependent on the quality of mothering occurring when the child is young.

"It can be hard because kids don't understand. When I'd leave, little Al would get mad and not talk to me. But I have to be happy, too. I wouldn't be a happy mother if I was staying home as a housewife." That is Olympic gold medal runner Valerie Brisco-Hooks speaking to a *New York Times* interviewer. She is not alone in her belief that motherhood is a hurdle that must be jumped in order to find real fulfillment.

The Labor Department says that nearly half of the nation's married women with children one year old or younger are in the labor force. The figure jumped from 24 percent in 1970 to 46.8 percent by the end of 1984. Of married women with children under eighteen, three-fifths are now working, a staggering number that has brought with it a profound sociological impact.

While some of these women obviously must work in order to survive, others work for different reasons. Regardless of the reason, the impact on families, particularly children, is severe.

Psychologist Dr. James Dobson advises the White House and the Pentagon on family life. He has sold more than four million books on family relationships and his "Focus on the Family" radio program is heard on 640 stations in eight countries.

Dobson says a child may suffer permanent emotional damage from an exhausted lifestyle when there is no full-time homemaker in the house.

Numerous studies have shown that children who are shuttled

from one baby sitter to another are different from what they would be otherwise. Research has consistently demonstrated that the mother-child relationship is especially vital during the first three years of life and that there is no substitute for the bonding that occurs between generations during that time. The Harvard preschool study revealed that a child's future intellectual capacity and emotional security are largely dependent on the quality of mothering occurring when the child is young.

Numerous studies have found, notes Dobson, that children "thrown into group situations too early" incline toward peer-dependency and insecurity as they move through childhood.

Further, the households of two-income families tend to be more chaotic and less organized than those with a homemaker on duty. The stress level of every family member is increased in a home where time is limited for recreation and relaxed conversation.

Dobson believes there are several questions mothers who have a choice about whether to work should ask themselves: 1) To whom shall I submit the task of guiding the unfolding process of development during the years when dramatic changes are occurring in my children? 2) Who will care enough to make the investment if every day my husband and I are too busy for the job? 3) What group-oriented facility can possibly substitute for the individual attention and love my child needs? 4) Who will represent values and beliefs and be ready to answer our child's questions during his peak period of interest? 5) To whom will I surrender the prime-time experiences of his day?

Says Dobson, "I worry about a nation that calls homemaking unrewarding, unfulfilling, and boring."

The 1909 White House Conference on Children had it right when it concluded, "Home life is the highest and finest product of civilization. . . . Except in unusual circumstances, the home should not be broken up for reasons of poverty." It was in the 1920s that a new ideology of "social parenting" began to take shape in America. This has led us to the "modern family," no better represented than in the movie, "Irreconcilable Differences."

In the film Casey Brodsky, age ten, is divorcing her parents. Says Casey, "If I'm not going to be totally nuts when I grow up,

I'd better get out while I still have a chance." Mom and Dad are so involved with personal ambitions that they don't have the time and energy to give Casey the warmth and affection that all children need. In the end they realize this and make a new start. In real life not everyone comes to such a realization.

As we relentlessly pursue "happiness," we would do well to remember what C. S. Lewis wrote: "We have no right to happiness. We have only an obligation to do our duty." It is in doing that duty that ultimate happiness is to be found.

January 29, 1985

FIFTY - SEVEN

WHEN YOU CARE
ENOUGH

. . . Who ever thought we would ever see racy cards from staid old Hallmark?

The Hallmark card company, whose slogan, "When you care enough to send the very best," has made its way into the fabric of American tradition along with motherhood and apple pie, is seventy-five years old this year. And how is the company observing its diamond anniversary? By coming out with a new line of cards in an effort to keep up with the times.

A Hallmark press release notes the recent sociological changes that have resulted from both spouses working in 42 percent of marriages, a large increase in the number of single-parent households, a 50 percent divorce rate, and "changing male role models."

"From this," says Hallmark, "has come the need for more tailored, less emotional cards suitable for business situations . . . love relationships [which, from looking at the cards I would conclude do not necessarily lead to marriage and are very suggestive], divorce cards, and invitations for a woman to send to invite a man for an evening for two."

I asked the company to send me some of these new cards so I could see, as a happily married, well-adjusted male, what I am missing.

One of the divorce cards says on the outside, "Starting over isn't easy." Inside we find the basal reader approach, with one sentence on each of several pages leading to the sender's assurance of "how much I care."

Another divorce card is more direct. It shows a cartoon figure cutting a ball and chain from his leg and expressing him-self, "AAAAHHHH!" Inside, the card says, "Free at last. Con-gratulations."

Some of the cards are definitely in tune with the times. One shows a guy sitting on top of a computer. A heart is on the com-puter screen. Open it up and it says, "I'd sure like to access your program!"

And who ever thought we would ever see racy cards from old Hallmark? One is in the shape of a liquor bottle with a little bear saying, "Remember: Sex and alcohol don't mix!" Inside it says, "Set your drink down first!" I wonder why they use so many ex-clamation points?

For the ethereal-minded, there's a card with a foxy-looking woman and a man with his shirt unbuttoned. Open it up and it says, "Maybe you're not good for me and maybe I'm not good for you — but when have we ever done what's good for us?" Don't you love it?

For the feminist, Hallmark suggests this card. The scene on the outside is a chemistry lab. Two of the scientists are women. There is a bewildered-looking man, who is obviously not in charge of his life, much less the lab. The card says, "If they can make penicillin out of moldy cheese . . ." and you open it up to read, "Maybe we can make men out of the low-lifes in this town." This one's a must for Phil Donahue and Marlo.

There's even a pet sympathy card to send to the owners of Rover who has passed on to that big dog house in the sky.

I would like to get in on this trend, because there is obviously a lot of money to be made.

Here are some of my suggestions: How about a card for all of those one hundred thousand Democrats the Republicans are trying to convert in time for the 1986 elections? On the outside would be a donkey with a removable tail, which you could pin on the elephant pictured inside?

They could create a card with a closet on it for the sender to announce he is coming out of.

Prayer-in-school advocates could send to students cards con-taining a prayer that could be easily hidden in a history book so the ACLU wouldn't find out.

Those Americans engaged in espionage could send the

Soviets a spy card containing top-secret information.

Bleeding-heart liberals could buy edible cards to address to the poor, paying for them out of their own pockets and thus ending welfare programs.

One problem the Hallmark folks may have with these cards. They say that some card production begins eighteen to twenty-four months before the cards actually become available. Even while hurrying to catch up with the times, they may have fallen behind the times. The company's sample cards arrived at my office on the same day I tore an article out of the newspaper that was headlined, "Rediscovering the family: Wedding bells signal a new appreciation of old virtues."

June 16, 1985

FIFTY-EIGHT

SERPENT'S TEETH AND THANKLESS CHILDREN

"I thought I was a good father. I tried to be a good mother." How many parents have literally cried themselves to sleep uttering those phrases?

Ronald Reagan has stirred many emotions during his presidency: pride, anger, joy, frustration, envy. But during the recent Barbara Walters interview with the President and Mrs. Reagan, I felt a new emotion. I felt sympathy for the President and his wife.

Sympathy for the two most famous people and the most powerful man in the world? Yes, for no matter how famous or successful one is, the fact that one's children did not turn out well can be like a nagging toothache that cannot be ignored.

Excuse me, Mr. President, but I never did believe you when you said that the book written by your daughter, Patti Davis, was just a small curiosity and that you and Mrs. Reagan felt it was "interesting fiction." Your interview with Barbara Walters confirmed my parental suspicions. You, like me, can be blessed or hurt by how your children behave and what they think of you.

And so, in the lament so familiar to every parent of a child gone astray, you said, "I thought I was a good father," and Mrs. Reagan said, "I tried to be a good mother." The only parental utterance more familiar than those lines is by Shakespeare, who had King Lear say, "How sharper than a serpent's tooth it is to have a thankless child."

You admitted that you had been hurt, angry, and annoyed at the less than flattering description of your roles as parents in the thinly veiled novel. And who wouldn't be had they been described as a father "who's interested in his political career to the exclusion of his children, and a mother who was a clothes horse, and so protective of the father that she won't let the kids give their own feelings."

Obviously, Patti Davis has learned to overcome restraint for fun and profit.

But let's put the shoe on the other foot. The Reagans have shown considerable restraint over their public comments about a daughter who shares none of their values and a son whose biggest claim to fame is that he danced in his underwear on network television. Children can only blame their parents for the sins visited on them for so long. Ultimately the children must take charge of their own lives and be accountable for their own decisions.

How about some sympathy for the Reagans? Without them, no one would care what Ron Jr. did, in or out of his underwear, which seems an appropriate mode of dress considering his articles in *Playboy* magazine. And as dopey as "Good Morning America" gets, even ABC would not hire Ron Reagan to ask such penetrating questions as, "Have you ALWAYS wanted to be a singer?" had he not been the President's son.

And as for Patti Davis, she might, if she really worked at it, hope to do PR for the nuclear freeze movement. She surely would not be on the Phil Donahue show to help Phil put down her parents!

But back to the two lines that put the Reagans on the same level as all of us: "I thought I was a good father. I tried to be a good mother." How many parents have literally cried themselves to sleep uttering those phrases?

If there was a worse time to rear children in our country, I don't know when it might have been. Every social evil known to humanity seems to have converged on the end of the twentieth century. The Reagans are not alone among the rich and famous. The son of Geraldine Ferarro and John Zaccaro is facing drug charges at Middlebury College. And what about Brown University, where allegedly a prostitution ring involving the children of presumably caring parents has recently been discovered?

I know a man who tried to be a good father and a woman who thought she was a good mother. Two of their children rejected their values and engaged in behavior that broke their parents' hearts. For nearly three years the parents anguished over their children's lifestyles, but they slowly came to realize that their children, whom they loved, were individuals and ultimately responsible for what they made out of their own lives. And so, they continue to love them, but have set them free as adults to earn the benefits or suffer the consequences of their chosen behavior.

It may still hurt to think about their transgressions. But releasing them in this way is all that any of us who are parents, including the most powerful man in the world and his wife, can do.

March 30, 1986

FIFTY-NINE

ANYTHING GOES

. . . Pornographically cheapened sex is a direct attack on family stability.

When Cole Porter wrote the title song to his 1930s musical, "Anything Goes," he probably did not have in mind the kind of material that is supposedly protected by the First Amendment in the 1980s: "In olden days a glimpse of stocking was looked on as something shocking, now heaven knows! Anything goes."

The critics of the Attorney General's Commission on Pornography have had a disinformation field day with leaked bits and pieces of the report, representing it as something it is not, in hopes of derailing any subsequent action that might curtail the spread of this social disease.

The ACLU and liberal publications like *The New Republic* would have us believe that the real targets of the commission are the airbrushed pages of *Playboy* and *Penthouse*. While some commission members would, indeed, categorize these magazines as pornographic, they are mild compared to books, magazines, and films that portray torture, bestiality, rape, mutilation, sado-masochistic activity, and other acts so vile that even their description is enough to turn one's stomach. Yet, it is all there in the nineteen-hundred-page report, which refers to the depiction of such actions as the "mainstream" of contemporary pornography. As one commission member noted, "To look at this material is like going through a sewer in a glass-bottom boat."

While the commission's report does call for some new controls on pornography, it is most critical of those who have refused to enforce laws already on the books, laws that have passed constitutional muster. And the report again underscores that organized crime finances many of its activities with the $4 billion it earns annually from pornography.

While a commission majority sought to link more violent forms of pornography with violence against women and children, there is an even greater impact that may be harder to analyze from a scientific cause-effect standpoint, but nonetheless ought to be of paramount concern.

Pornography's perversion of the sex act cheapens sex and reduces human beings to behavior from which animals would flee. Humans are converted into sexual machines to be used and manipulated for the immediate gratification of sick minds.

More importantly, it can be asserted with some degree of credibility that pornographically cheapened sex is a direct attack on family stability in that it weakens this critical adhesive in the marriage relationship.

A man who becomes addicted to pornography—and the word addiction is used by one of the commission members, who also says that such material is progressive in nature—tends to become obsessed by his need, and thus it can interfere with the normal sexual relationship between husband and wife.

Commission critics have tried to convince us that most of the members began their task with their minds already made up about pornography.

Not so, said one member, Dr. Park Elliot Dietz, a noted psychiatrist.

"The morality of pornography was the farthest thing from my mind," said Dr. Deitz. "Thus, I was astonished to find that by the final meeting of the commission, pornography had become a matter of moral concern to me. While other commissioners may have learned things about the dark side of life that they had never known, I remembered something about the higher purposes of life and of humanity's aspirations that I had forgotten during too many years working on the dark side. I therefore conclude my remarks with statements on morality and on freedom that would have seemed foreign to me not many months ago."

The commission's recommendations for control of pornography do not violate the First Amendment, as critics charge. In the words of the report, ". . . not every use of words, pictures, or a printing press automatically triggers protection by the First Amendment. . . . As Justice Holmes stated in 1919, 'The First Amendment . . . cannot have been, and obviously was not, intended to give immunity for every possible use of language.' "

People magazine headlined its article on the commission's report, "The Shame of America." It is an apt title.

A society has a right, indeed an obligation to decide for itself the minimum standards by which it will live. The Supreme Court has upheld such a right in rulings on obscenity. It is now up to the people's representatives to decide through their state and federal legislators and through the offices of their local prosecutors what they want done with the findings of this report.

July 10, 1986

PART FIVE

RE-CHARTING
THE COURSE

SIXTY

SEX, THE "RIGHT" WAY

No law, including the law requiring that seat belts be worn, ensures universal conformity. Laws are designed to set a minimum standard of excellence.

The driver of the car picking me up at the airport for my first visit to California this year tells me to be sure to fasten my seat belt. A new mandatory seat belt law took effect not long ago, and the state wants to make sure that I am protected, whether I want to be or not.

It is one of a lengthening list of laws, rules, and regulations that attempt to force us to conform to what is considered to be a practice we too might consider wise, had we the omniscience of government authorities. The list includes age limits for consuming alcoholic beverages, driving automobiles, and attending certain movies. It encompasses contracts, speed limits, leaf burning, and where carry-on baggage must be placed on airplanes.

Only in the area of sex does there remain a reticence to tell people what is best for them. It is not that we lack evidence that premature sexual encounters often bring consequences at least as serious, if not more so, than those the other laws are enacted to prevent. It is rather that we lack the will to suggest limits (other than rape — what playwright Budd Schulberg once wrote is "the friendliest thing two people can do").

Perhaps we fear being labeled "puritanical," though the Puritans seem to have had fewer problems than their descendants, particularly in the area of what used to be called "illicit sex" prior to the stripping of those words of their meaning.

A decade ago the anti-ERA leader, Phyllis Schlafly, was roundly booed and vilified when she told campus audiences that the best contraceptive, indeed the best guarantee against venereal disease, was a simple formula: one man-one woman-one lifetime.

Not as many laugh at such a formula today, in part because of the serious consequences of sex outside the bounds of heterosexual marriage, and in part because those who mock puritanism have failed to come up with a better formula.

In nearly every other area of human life, there is a preference for applying formulas that work to solve problems. Only in the area of humanity's most powerful and personal emotion, the sex drive, is "what works" never the beginning point and, in fact, is frequently never a part of the equation at all.

Why is this?

Perhaps the answer can be found in a newspaper ad for an automobile the manufacturer hopes to persuade me to buy. The headline says, "Fall in Love Without Paying the Price." A better summation of contemporary attitudes about sex could not be found. It is a type of moral shoplifting. We want the goods, but we don't wish to pay the price. Is it any wonder, then, that some women complain of a commitment crisis among the men they know?

When we are caught in our pursuit of pleasure without commitment, as in the case of unwanted pregnancies or venereal disease, we still do not acknowledge the existence of a standard to which we ought to conform. Rather, we ask that our failure to adhere to such a standard be overlooked in favor of an abortion or a vaccine so that we can continue as before.

In California, as in other states, police officers will hand out a ticket for failure to conform to the mandatory seat belt law. It is too much to expect (and impossible to enforce) that tickets be handed to persons engaging in sex outside of marriage, but it does occur to me that there could, as a starting point, be a mandatory curriculum in the schools to counteract the drumbeat of sensuality that assaults the senses through the media.

Instead of taking an approach of exposing students to all of their sexual options, as if all are equal and none is to be preferred, what would be wrong with forcefully telling them not to engage in sex until marriage and warning of the consequences if they do?

Not possible, you say? They will do it anyway, you assert?

Not necessarily. No law, including the law requiring that seat belts be worn, ensures universal conformity. Laws are designed to set a minimum standard of expectation. That is what is missing in the sex equation. It is such a standard that would again delineate between freedom and license.

Arriving back in Washington, I noticed a large ad displayed next to the baggage claim. It says, "125,000 junior high students flunked this simple test last year." The ad is for a home pregnancy test kit. If so many are flunking the test, perhaps they need a tutor in self-control instead of a pregnancy test kit or the increasingly popular birth control clinic on school grounds.

After all, if they can be taught by the cultural drumbeat to engage in premature sex, why can't they be taught by a different drummer to abstain for now?

May 1, 1986

SIXTY-ONE

CHILDREN IN POVERTY: WHOSE FAULT?

The government at the federal, state, and local level needs to resurrect a long-dormant word. It is the word "no."

In announcing the findings of a congressional study that says that 22.2 percent of the nation's children now live in poverty, Rep. Charles Rangel (D-N.Y.) predictably blamed the Reagan Administration's budget policies.

"The Reagan Administration needs to recognize that its policies are having a very detrimental and long-lasting effect on our children who live in poverty," said Rangel. "One can hardly expect our youth to grow up and become productive members of society if they do not have a stable home life, proper shelter, and sufficient amounts of food and clothing."

Though Rangel's solution to the problem (more government spending) has proved a dismal failure, the order in which he places this three-horned dilemma is correct. If one does not have a stable home life, one is less likely to have proper shelter, food, and clothing.

So the question is, how can a stable home life best be achieved? Certainly not by more federal programs.

In fact, says Robert L. Woodson, chairman of the Council for a Black Economic Agenda, "many current programs intended to assist black families are in fact undermining them."

According to the congressional study, "never-married mothers present the most severe child poverty problem (three out of four children of such mothers are poor) and their ranks are growing. In 1980, almost one-fifth of births were to unwed mothers, 48 percent of black births and 11 percent of white births. If the incidence of never-married mothers had not increased from 1969 to 1975, it is estimated that the overall poverty rate might have been 5 percent lower in 1979."

Clearly, at least to those who can see out of the federal program forest, the answer is not more tax money that sustains people in their poverty and encourages, or at least makes it easier, for others to follow suit.

Realizing that there is "nothing new under the sun," I would propose two approaches to solving the poverty problem in America.

First, the government at the federal, state, and local level needs to resurrect a long-dormant word. It is the word "no." Government has an interest in establishing and helping to maintain a moral water table. It can do much to promote chastity among teenagers and commitment in marriage. A continuation of the current trend in which everyone does what is right in his or her own eyes will perpetuate the poverty problem and lead to other social anomalies. Teaching the young to say no to premarital sex and no to divorce is in keeping with the preamble to the Constitution, which speaks of "promoting the GENERAL welfare" (not everybody's welfare, as is currently the case, and which in fact dilutes the welfare of all of us).

Laugh if you will, but what other approach has proven as effective? Chastity until marriage is still the only foolproof way to prevent unwanted pregnancies, venereal disease, and the social fallout that accompanies them. The reason it hasn't worked on a broad scale is similar to the reason we have so much difficulty getting people to stop smoking. One branch of government tells us that smoking is dangerous to our health while another branch subsidizes the tobacco growers. Kids are getting conflicting messages from the culture. No wonder they are confused.

The second proposal has to do with the responsibility of churches and synagogues for the poor among us.

When Congress wrote tax exemptions into the Internal Revenue Code, it was felt that religious institutions should be exempt from paying taxes because it was assumed that they provide spiritual and material benefits to the nation that government could not or should not attempt to provide.

Several years ago, the office of Sen. Mark Hatfield (R-Ore.)

took a survey found that if every church and synagogue in America cared for one family on public assistance, the welfare rolls would be eliminated.

Let a survey be conducted that matches the poor with the places of worship in their area. The churches and synagogues would then be contacted and their support enlisted. Many churches and synagogues, particularly the ones that believe in faith AND works, are already doing this job. Many others, if the Hatfield study is correct, are not. It seems to me that if religious bodies enjoy a government benefit such as tax exemption, they ought to prove that they are worthy of that benefit by helping the poor and thus easing the burden of government.

More government spending is an easy way out for politicians, but for the poor it is no way out at all.

May 30, 1985

MEDIA BASHING: WHAT NEXT?

Liberals understand all too well that a powerful idea is worth more than a lot of money. Money only buys things that ultimately must become obsolete, but ideas fuel revolutions that change the course of history.

Now that CBS has successfully repurchased enough of its stock to forestall a takeover by Ted Turner, those concerned about what they regard as a one-sided presentation of the news have two choices. They can either continue to whine and complain like spoiled brats who are kept from playing with the big boys' toys, or they can get serious and really do something about it.

Unfortunately, the initial signs indicate that more tantrums and statements of the obvious will follow.

Fairness in Media, the group that started the media acquisition rush last January, says it plans to keep on going. The group, spearheaded by Sen. Jesse Helms (R-N.C.), which urged conservatives to buy CBS stock so they could "become Dan Rather's boss," will buy television spots on Turner Broadcasting System, Inc., excoriating CBS's news coverage as "rather biased." Why don't they also buy some time to advertise that cows don't fly?

Terry Dolan of the National Conservative Foundation has launched a campaign to raise $1 million "to educate the American public to view [the media] with a jaundiced eye." Dolan says the group will purchase TV and radio spots and newspaper ads to convince the American people to take what the media has to say with a grain of salt.

All right. Let us say that these groups are successful with their campaigns. The TV and radio spots are aired, the newspaper ads are printed. Then what? What do they really expect to happen?

Can we expect ABC's Sam Donaldson to fall on his knees on the White House lawn during one of his smirking reports about the president and plead for forgiveness? Will conservatives be satisfied if Sam promises to reactivate his membership in the Young Republican Club of El Paso, Texas? Will Dan Rather, overcome with patriotism, praise the President as the greatest leader in history and ask for the privilege of narrating a filmed biography of life? Hardly. And, by the way, if all of this did happen, would liberals then charge there was too much bias in the media? You bet they would. David Brinkley once said that something is biased only if you disagree with it.

No, all that this latest round of media-bashing will do is raise a lot more money for groups that really have no intention of accomplishing much more than raising money. With the exception of Ted Turner, these cry-babies would not know how to run a professional news operation that attracts viewers and makes a profit if they had to.

What about the alternative of having an impact on the bias? I have spoken with an editor at one major newspaper and with a publisher at another about the seeming ideological imbalance in journalism. Each told me he or she would run more conservative columnists if there were more good ones who could write. Doesn't sound to me as if their so-called bias has affected their professional judgement.

But even if you grant that there is bias (and we are all biased to some extent — what the critics are actually complaining about is a lack of fairness or balance), why are there not more conservative young people in the journalism schools and working their way up through the ranks of small-town newspapers and TV stations?

I'll tell you what I think is the answer to that question. My own experience has shown me that many conservatives do not have a well enough developed world view. They do not understand that history is a battle of ideas. They are not willing to sacrifice the MBA at Harvard for the toil and often low pay (with the exception of those in Dan Rather's category) of the journalism profession. When they have made their fortunes in business, they would rather invest in oil wells and stock than in the ideological health of their country. They hold a lot of meetings, usually to talk about the "liberal threat," but they do nothing.

Liberals understand all too well that a powerful idea is worth more than a lot of money. Money only buys things that ultimately must become obsolete, but ideas fuel revolutions that change the course of history.

After the cursing of the darkness has been completed, one is still left with darkness. But light always dispels darkness and if only a few of those conservatives who are upset by what they see on television and read in the newspapers would put their money where their ideology is, what a bright world this would be. Until then, I am afraid that many of my conservative brethren will be regarded as a bunch of cry-babies.

August 8, 1985

SIXTY-THREE

THE HUNGER ISSUE

If donations alone could end hunger, why do we still have the hungry with us?

Hunger has re-emerged as a subject of some concern for the entertainment industry and a few others who need the attention the press always gives to those who express "concern" for the starving. Hunger is the ultimate guilt-producing issue, though fund-raising for AIDS victims seems to be catching on fast. Who can resist, who can criticize, the malnourished and disease-ravaged child whose face we have seen scores of times in news footage or on television specials. The narrator inevitably urges us to help "solve" the hunger problem simply by calling a toll-free number and making a pledge.

If world hunger could be solved with a John Denver song or a Cicely Tyson homily (both have recently been in the news urging that more be done to feed the world), it would have disappeared long ago. But hunger has not vanished for the same reason that two aspirin and a phone call to the doctor in the morning do not cure cancer. They are the wrong prescriptions.

The basic cause of hunger is not lack of available food or lack of compassion by Americans, the poorest of whom are rich by the standards of the rest of the world.

This Halloween UNICEF ought to be collecting money to pass out tracts favoring democratic capitalism along with the food, for it is only when governments are restructured in areas where hunger persists that hunger will be brought under control.

To hear people like John Denver and Cicely Tyson tell it, the United States and its people are not doing enough to solve the hunger problem. Yet, the United Sates is spending $1 billion in

Africa alone to help the starving survive and it provides one-half of all food aid in the world today.

Secretary of Agriculture John Block tells me, "Just to make people dependent on an indefinite handout is not the right answer. They need to develop their economies and that means making reforms." Capitalism may not have the "sex appeal" of hungry faces and pleading voices, but it is distinctive in one important way. It works.

Block points to those nations that have deliberately kept their prices artificially low. This has meant that Third World farmers have no incentive to raise food for their people.

Secretary Block points to nations that feed bread to their hogs as just one example of agricultural theories that have helped created hungry citizens. He says the United States is prepared to share its technologies with other nations and is, in fact, doing so with some, but that this must be coupled with a willingness by other countries to help themselves.

While Block says he is grateful for such projects as Live Aid (though he says he has no idea where the money has gone and how much has actually helped the hungry), "our ultimate goal must be to help nations with hungry people to become self-reliant. I didn't say 'self-sufficient' because some will not be able to produce all that they need, but if their economies are strengthened, they can buy what they cannot raise."

As for the Soviet Union, Block points out that their contribution to end hunger is so small it cannot be measured, but Soviet arms supplies to hungry nations, such as Ethiopia, are huge.

While certain singers and actresses are off on this latest guilt trip they might do well to remember the words of scholar and economic expert Michael Novak, who has written, "No better weapon against poverty, disease, illiteracy, and tyranny has yet been found than capitalism. The techniques, human skills, and changes of cultural habit necessary to expand the productive capacity of the earth have been pioneered by democratic capitalism. Its compassion for the material needs of humankind has not in history yet had a peer."

Capitalism compassionate? That is a totally new concept to the John Denvers and Cicely Tysons. If donations alone could end hunger, why do we still have the hungry with us?

To paraphrase the peace chants of the last decade: all we are saying is, give capitalism a chance.

October 27, 1985

SIXTY-FOUR

FREEDOM OF CHOICE

. . . If the choice is between education control and education excellence, the establishment will choose control every time.

Choice is a concept that is dear to the heart of my liberal friends. They sincerely believe that everyone should be free to do what is right in his own eyes. Only the narrowest of restrictions is to be tolerated, until it appears a choice might be made that veers away from the plan they have mapped out for the rest of us. In such instances, choice becomes unconstitutional.

Take the education of our children as an example. The Secretary of Education, William J. Bennett, has proposed a voucher system that would credit parents with $600 to be applied to whatever school they believe will best educate their children. This might be another public school closer to home, a religious or non-religious private school, or the same public school the child now attends.

The reaction to the plan by the education establishment demonstrates that if the choice is between education control and education excellence, the establishment will choose control every time.

The National Education Association's Mary Hatwood Futrell called the proposal a "sham" that would hurt public schools while making only a small dent on the tuition at most private schools.

The *New York Times* picked up on that theme and said the plan was a "cruel hoax," since the $600 voucher would come nowhere near paying what it says is the average inner-city parochial school tuition of $1,000.

Apparently the critics of the voucher system have not spoken with officials at the Archdiocese of Chicago. The Archdiocese commissioned a survey that asked 1,066 people, including non-Catholics and people from different income groups, for their views on private schools and tuition tax credits. The survey wanted to determine, among other things, what difference a voucher system would make in a family's choice to send their children to school.

Archdiocesan spokeswoman Sister Cathy Campbell says that 60 percent of those questioned who do not have their children in private schools would enroll them in those schools if tuition was not a problem.

Those with children in parochial schools were asked why they had placed them there. Four reasons were given: quality of education, better preparation for life (which Sister Campbell says means, among other things, a value-centered education that teaches the children right from wrong), the Catholic character of the school, and higher standards of behavior.

Responding to the criticism that $600 creates a "cruel hoax" for the poor, Sister Campbell says it is enough money for many families to bridge the gap between what they can pay and what they cannot afford. Often, she says, members of low-income families will pool their resources to educate a child. So, with contributions from Grandma, Uncle Everett, and Aunt Sue, junior gets the quality of education his family wants him to have and the government benefits by the production of a better citizen. Everybody wins, except those who fear losing control of the education establishment.

A top Department of Education official tells me that parents must request the voucher and that no child will be deprived of any services currently offered under programs for the educationally disadvantaged, regardless of what school his parents want him to attend.

Besides, the competition ought to be good for the education establishment. If monopolies were deemed bad for those who would own a newspaper and a television station in the same town, if AT&T had to be dismembered for the public good, why not break the grip of the NEA and the American Federation of Teachers from our children's brains?

There is a lot to be gained and not much to lose from at least giving the voucher idea a try. For once we could erect a sign outside the schools of our choice and be proud when we read, "Your tax dollars at work."

November 21, 1985

SIXTY-FIVE

NOT ENOUGH BABIES

Adoption is the short-term middle ground many have been searching for in the polarized abortion debate.

"And the Lord God said to Adam and Eve, 'Be fruitful and multiply, and replenish the Earth. . . .' "

It's a command that two million American couples are incapable of fulfilling. They are the childless couples who would be even more thankful during this special season if they were able to adopt a child.

They hope to take home one of the 142,000 to 160,000 children placed for adoption each year. For many of them, the wait can last as long as seven years.

At the same time, thousands of teen-age girls choose to keep babies they are emotionally, educationally, and financially unprepared to raise. And about 1.5 million babies are aborted each year —babies who would have been welcomed by childless couples.

A recent study by the National Committee for Adoption is revealing several ways. For one thing, the study refutes the contention of abortion advocates that people only want to adopt white, blond, blue-eyed children who are physically and mentally perfect; that other children have little chance of finding foster homes.

The committee study showed that more than one-fourth (27.6 percent) of all adoptions involve "special needs" children who are mentally or physically disabled.

There are several reasons for the shortage of adoptable babies. Many unmarried young women, thinking they are doing the courageous thing or that an infant will make their young lives happier, choose to keep children rather than place them for adoption by families better prepared to care for them.

A study by Dr. Christine Bachrach of the National Center for Health Statistics shows that where the child is born out of wedlock, "the young mother does better if she decides on adoption and the child certainly does better."

Annually, half a million women under the age of twenty-five have babies outside of marriage, but only 9 percent are ever placed for adoption. Half of these adoptable children are white and half are black, and 98 percent are classified as healthy infants.

Two other "cultural attitudes," often encouraged by so-called "pro-choicers" in the debate over human life, contribute to the limited number of adoptable babies. One is the attitude, "Oh, I couldn't give my baby away." This expression is offered shortly before (or shortly after) an abortion.

So, killing in secret is better than placing a child for adoption where some couple could provide everything the reluctant mother either cannot or does not wish to provide.

The second attitude is reflected in a movement I was not familiar with until William Pierce, president of the National Committee for Adoption, told me about it. It is an attitude promoted by a small but noisy group called "Concerned United Birth Parents."

In one of the "bibles" of the movement, called *Death by Adoption*, by Joss Shawyer of New Zealand, there is this: "As an abortion counselor, I have been in a position to compare the traumatic results of adoption with the comparatively simple remedy of early, safe abortion. In my view, there is no contest."

The opening sentence of this book says, "Adoption is a violent act, a political act of aggression towards a woman who has supposedly offended the sexual mores by committing the unforgivable act of not suppressing her sexuality and therefore keeping it for trading purposes through traditional marriage."

Pierce says many unwed mothers are never adequately informed of the adoption alternative. To expect an abortion clinic to recommend adoption would be like expecting a florist to say "in lieu of flowers."

Far too little has been written about the positive benefits of adoption. (The *Reader's Guide to Periodical Literature* has only two entries; one for transracial adoptions and the other related to the tearful stories of people searching for their natural parents, who were "forced" by their parents or by society to give up the child.)

Adoption is the short-term middle ground many have been searching for in the polarized abortion debate. That way, everybody wins. The unwed woman need not feel guilt, or face the uphill struggle of raising a child without adequate resources and support. Couples who cannot have children receive an enormous blessing, and "pro-choicers" can't complain.

November 28, 1985

SIXTY-SIX

DEMOCRACY IS OUR MOST IMPORTANT PRODUCT

While the debate continues over who is stronger militarily, the Soviet Union or the United States, there is no doubt that an "education gap" exists between the two countries.

When Ronald Reagan used to do commercials for the General Electric Company, he spoke their slogan with conviction: "At General Electric, PROGRESS is our most important product."

The Administration and Congress have finally gotten around to realizing that for the United States, democracy is our most important product, and that it is time to expand the effort to sell it abroad.

Now, under a new $3.8 million scholarship program sponsored by the United States Information Agency (USIA), more than 150 college students from seven Central American countries, including six from Nicaragua, have just arrived in the U.S., to "absorb some of our values," in the words of one official.

The elite from the nations of the world have long studied at American universities, but the USIA program is different because if focuses on poor students who have good aptitudes but few resources. Had the scholarship money not been available, say officials, these students might have gone to study in the Soviet Union instead.

While the debate continues over who is stronger militarily, the Soviet Union or the United States, there is no doubt that an "education gap" exists between the two countries. The Soviet interest in educating Central Americans has increased enormously since 1979, when only five hundred students were given scholarships to study in Russia. In 1983, the latest year for which figures are available, the Soviets took in 3,030 Central Americans while another 1,435 went to East European bloc countries to study.

The American response to the Soviet effort was puny by comparison. Only 226 students from Central America were enrolled in American universities in programs comparable to those in the Soviet Union. The approximately 6,200 other students from Central America who studied here were children of the wealthy who paid their own way.

House Majority Leader Jim Wright (D-Texas) had it right when he observed, "Rich students come to the United States; poor students go to the Soviet bloc countries on full scholarships." He might have added that Afghan children go to the Soviet Union as kidnap victims where they are forcibly enrolled in the rapidly growing "school of brainwashing."

Yes, a mind is a terrible thing to waste, and there is no place where it gets wasted faster than in the Soviet Union.

When one looks at Africa, a continent in more turmoil than the Central American region, the education picture is even bleaker. In 1982, thirty-seven thousand Africans received scholarships to study in the Soviet Union or Eastern bloc countries while only three thousand African students were awarded scholarships to study in America.

USIA officials say the newly arrived Central American students will study a range of subjects, including business, education, social sciences, natural sciences, engineering, and nutrition. But what they will be getting while they are here will go far beyond textbooks and classroom instruction. They will be able to see why democracy is the best system in the world, and it is hoped they will be able to take home with them a desire to keep their nations free (or in the case of Nicaragua, to see freedom restored) along with the tools they need to help them do it.

USIA spokesman Dick Carlson says the education imbalance between the Soviets and Americans should improve now that Congress has passed a law authorizing a worldwide scholarship program under USIA direction, beginning next year. Funding for the program has yet to be authorized, however, pending a study of the success of the current program in Central America.

For those who are concerned that the Central American students might find the U.S. to their liking and want to stay, the visas they carry specifically prohibit them from doing so.

The scholarship program for potential leaders of Central American nations is a fine idea. The only question is, why did we let the Soviets have this field to themselves for so long?

January 19, 1986

SIXTY-SEVEN

A MORE EFFECTIVE WAY TO ATTACK *AIDS* CRISIS

Amazingly this Administration, which has launched an all-out attack on smoking and which has proclaimed "just say no" as the solution to the drug problem, has not found an effective way to attack the AIDS crisis.

This is not a time for calm introspection about AIDS. As Mickey Kaus of *The New Republic* has written, this is a time for panic. Says Kaus, "To be blunt about it, what's more important, casual sex or avoiding a medical holocaust?"

Kaus gets to the heart of the matter when he speaks of the unfulfilled promises of the sexual liberation movement of the 1960s: "Today, none of us wants to admit that we made a mistake, that this wonderful experiment was an epic social blunder. . . ."

Yet, some voices still proclaim the "right" of those who wish to indulge in the behavior that puts people at risk to contract AIDS. Responsibility for doing something about the spread of AIDS has been conveniently transferred to government, which is supposed to discover a drug that will deliver the afflicted from the consequences of their actions.

Amazingly this Administration, which has launched an all-out attack on smoking and which has proclaimed "just say no" as the solution to the drug problem, has not found an effective way to attack the AIDS crisis. This is because the Administration and others in leadership positions have attempted to separate the disease from its moral roots. Indeed, it seems all types of behavior are justified now, and nothing is considered wrong except condemnation of wrongdoing.

So, instead of condemning the behavior that places individuals at risk for contracting AIDS, those in leadership positions institute "education" programs that attempt to teach people, including junior and senior high school students, how to have "safe sex." In California a bill has been introduced in the legislature which would require school districts to present AIDS prevention films to students in grades seven through twelve. Among the proposed films to be shown is one that depicts the varying risks of vaginal, oral, and anal sex, and intravenous drug use. Apparently condoms, not self-control, are to be our salvation.

There is a fundamental dishonesty in the campaign against AIDS. Politicians, journalists, and some medical experts are reluctant to emphasize that only limited forms of sexual behavior offer guarantees against infection with the AIDS virus. For example, a *Washington Post* writer says that AIDS may force us to reconsider the "quaint" notion of fidelity, implying that fornication is the norm.

U.S. News and World Report said in a recent cover story on AIDS that it is no longer "their" disease, it is now "our" disease. Well, it is not MY disease.

If you do not inject drugs, and are chaste until marriage and faithful within the marital bond, your chance of getting AIDS is reduced to almost nil. This is the message that the Reagan Administration ought to be shouting from the housetops. Anything less, such as handing out condoms, will have no more effect than passing out surgical masks would have had in curtailing smallpox.

If the sexual drumbeat in movies, popular records, and television has brought us to the precipice, why can't a drumbeat of a different sort carry us back to safety? It can, if those in politics, medicine, and education set the right cadence.

January 22, 1987

SIXTY - EIGHT

OUR OWN MAY DAY

While the American left urges talks with the Sandinista Communists, it cannot give one example where talking to such people has led to a free society with free elections.

The most intriguing story to come out of the recent meeting in Grenada between President Reagan and the prime ministers of ten Caribbean nations did not make it on the television networks or in the major newspapers, because most correspondents were already filing their stories when it happened.

But not Mutual Radio's Jim Slade, who paid attention when a State Department spokesman offered a briefing on the private discussion between the President and the prime ministers.

While others were busy calling their bureaus, Slade says the State Department spokesman related that as the leaders began talking about politics, the subject of Haiti and its recently deposed "president for life," Jean-Claude Duvalier, came up.

The department spokesman said some of the leaders urged President Reagan to "get busy and fill in the vacuum that exists in Haiti before Castro does." They also told the President, according to Slade's recounting of the spokesman's briefing, "Whatever you choose to do, we will support you. But do it quickly."

Such urgings come at a time when the State Department is still debating (and Congress must ultimately decide) just what form any future aid to Haiti should take. The Caribbean leaders also seemed unsure of what the Haitian military might do if left too long without a clear indication of the direction in which the United States would like it to go.

The American Left hates "adventurism" by the United States almost as much as it hates any suggestion that it is playing into Communist hands. And so, in the various news accounts of the

President's trip to Grenada, one could observe how the liberal writers and the politicians they quoted tried to dim the glow of the "Brezhnev doctrine"—which states that once a nation goes Communist, it will remain Communist.

Some stories tried to diminish the significance of the U.S. invasion by citing the high unemployment figures and weak economy in Grenada. Full employment is apparently more important to liberals than freedom. No Grenadian was asked whether he would rather have a state-supplied job and no freedom, or be out of work but have the freedom to pursue happiness and enjoy the blessings of liberty while searching for a job.

Other stories suggested that the military operation was tainted by "overkill." Seven thousand American troops assaulted the 133-square-mile island in October, 1983. But overkill is better than the underkill that produced the Bay of Pigs disaster. A little more "overkill" in Cuba, and the island nation would be free today, and probably Nicaragua, too, and El Salvador would not be struggling with Cuban and Soviet-backed guerilla warfare.

What we ought to be observing is a Western version of the Communist "May Day" parades. Every year, tanks and troops fill the streets of Moscow and other Communist capitals to celebrate the subjugation and imprisonment of 40 percent of the planet under the hammer and sickle.

To be sure, the United States has July 4, but that is a date on which we celebrate OUR freedom. What remains of the free world ought to have an annual joint celebration of freedom that could also show the rest of the world what it's missing.

While the American Left urges talks with the Sandinista Communists, it cannot give one example where talking to such people has led to a free society with free elections. The Communists use talk and negotiations to weaken American resolve and hold out the promise of "peace" while they continue grinding ahead on the battlefield.

The President is right to keep up the strong rhetoric against the Sandinistas and the Cubans. Congress now ought to help him match his bark with more military and economic bite, and it can start by giving military aid to the freedom fighters in Nicaragua. This is the only "talk" that the Soviets take seriously. Any other kind of talk they reserve for fools.

February 27, 1986

SIXTY-NINE

HEF TAKES A BIG GULP

If all the good people stopped complaining and actually DID something about some of our social ills, maybe they would bring change faster than waiting for the courts and legislatures to take an interest in the problem.

Hugh Hefner celebrated his sixtieth birthday recently and television pictures showed exactly what might be expected; lots of young women; lots of booze; lots of laughs.

But the laughs may be fewer now that Southland Corporation, owner of 7-Eleven, the nation's largest convenience store chain, has announced it will no longer sell *Playboy, Penthouse*, and other magazines we used to call "dirty" before dirt became a relative word. It is the latest of several recent setbacks for the Playboy empire, including legal problems with casinos and a decline in magazine sales.

The sexual revolution has ended and Hugh Hefner, the general who led the charge, is suddenly without an army. To be precise, the volunteer army of those who subscribed to the Playboy philosophy has been devastated by divorce, depression, and venereal disease, and few soldiers remain to fight the battles. In fact, the battles against chastity and faithfulness in marriage have been won. Trouble is, in the "peace" that followed, the people who fought the battle weren't any happier.

There is a lesson to be learned from this affair (pardon the expression). The decision by Southland to dump *Playboy* and other magazines came without a court decision or a legislative act. It is not ALWAYS necessary to turn to lawmakers or to judges to change social mores or store policies. In fact, change can sometimes be achieved more rapidly by boycotts or threats of boycotts, than by legislation or court decisions.

It was Edmund Burke who observed, "All that is necessary

for evil to triumph is for good men to do nothing." A lot of good men and women decided to do something to stem the growing $7 billion-a-year pornography industry. Instead of pinning their hopes on government, these good people decided to take matters into their own hands and use an even greater power: economics. Simply put, they said, "We won't tell you to stop publishing these magazines (which, in fact, they had tried unsuccessfully to do before). We are just not going to spend our money where they are sold."

This strategy worked. Now the giant 7-Eleven chain, with 8,100 stores, accounting for what a *Playboy* official has said is 20 percent of the magazine's total sales, has joined more than nine thousand other convenience stores in refusing to sell such magazines.

It is a marvelous strategy, which completely bypasses First Amendment "purists" who think that the Founders wanted to tolerate anything in the name of a free press. Nothing has been banned, and the rights of those who are offended by this material, when all they want is a jug of milk or a loaf of bread, are protected.

One wonders how many other social blights might be cured if good people were delivered from their apathy. How many abortions might be prevented if more people picketed the clinics and helped women in crisis pregnancy situations? How much television could be improved if good people stopped watching the sleazy and the dopey and wrote letters to the networks and their sponsors? How many schools might improve if more good people attended PTA and school board meetings?

To be sure, laws are necessary, but they are not always the most effective way to address every problem. If all of the good people stopped complaining and actually DID something about some of our social ills, maybe they would bring change faster than waiting for the courts and legislatures to take an interest in the problems.

That's what the picketers and the boycotters did with Southland Corporation. Now a lot of people will have something for which to give thanks . . . to heaven and to 7-Eleven.

April 17, 1986

SEVENTY

LINK LIVES,
NOT JUST HANDS

How many of the hungry and homeless are being fed and housed by those who bash Reagan Administration policies?

If the road to hell is paved with good intentions, then enough asphalt has been accumulated by Hands Across America and other "aid" events to build an eight-lane superhighway to perdition.

These events, while noble in purpose, serve only to assuage the guilt of one group and transfer that guilt to another group, which opposes more government programs that have failed to end poverty.

As Richard Krawieck, a volunteer worker in homeless shelters, noted in a recent *USA Today* column, "Hands Across America [was] a party for the privileged to celebrate their concern for the less privileged. It's a way for middle and upperclass folk who don't really want to face particular situations of poverty to pretend they're being compassionate while washing their hands of any personal responsibility."

The massive effort to end starving in Ethiopia reduced the rate of death, but not the cause. Despite efforts to convince the world that drought was the cause of starvation, the former head of Ethiopia's food relief effort, Dawit Wolde Giorgis, who has defected to the West, told the *New York Times* that it was primarily the economic policies of Ethiopia's Marxist government that were responsible for the mass starvation.

"We called it a drought problem," said Dawit, "but it was more a policy problem. . . . If there is no change in our policies, there will always be millions of hungry people in Ethiopia."

It is a change in policy that is needed to deal with the homeless and hungry in America. The Reagan Administration has begun to change by rejecting what I call the "McDonalds philosophy" of "we do it all for you." Now it is increasingly up to individual Americans to do it for their fellow men and women.

Not even "Hands Across America" can tell us how many hungry and homeless there are in the country. But there are far fewer than the number who held hands on Memorial Day weekend. What if a percentage of the hand-holders had each extended a helping hand to one homeless and/or hungry person? If they would not do it out of compassion, perhaps they might benefit from a tax break, provided that the person being helped does not return to public assistance within a specified time.

What if all of those celebrities, who are millionaires many times over, had used some of their wealth to help a homeless person find a home and feed a hungry person and then assist him in finding the means to provide for himself? It is one thing for actor Martin Sheen to play the role of homeless advocate Mitch Snyder on television. It is quite another for him to play such a role in real life and bring a poor person to dinner at his house and let him spend the night.

Have we not heard and understood the axiom that he who gives a man a fish feeds him for a day, but he who teaches a man how to fish helps him feed himself for a lifetime?

How many of the hungry and homeless are being fed and housed by those who bash Reagan Administration policies? Compassion is not asking the government to care for the poor, though government has a role to play. Compassion is seeing the need and meeting it yourself.

The reason why "Live Aid," "Farm Aid," "Hands Across America," and similar events will not provide long-term solutions to the problems they seek to address is they are fundamentally anonymous and impersonal exercises. If people knew the names and histories of those they were helping, if they could meet a needy person, the personal contact would create a bond from which real help would flow.

The late Robert Kennedy once observed that "to ignore the potential of private enterprise is to fight the war on poverty with a single platoon while great armies are left to stand aside."

Rep. Jack Kemp (R-N.Y.), the biggest apostle of free enterprise as a means of eliminating poverty, has called for a "second
war, or what we hope will be a successful war, on poverty. What
would a new war on poverty be like? Our strategy focuses on
three major facets: creating jobs, strengthening the neighborhood, and providing schools and education."

Such proposals may not be as "sexy" as mega-events like
"Hands Across America," but they have one advantage that the
mega-events do not have. They have a better chance of working.

May 29, 1986

SEVENTY-ONE

THE CRACK CRISIS

It is not enough to lock up the dealers and users. The users must be helped so that they will not provide repeat business for the dealers.

New York Mayor Edward Koch has proposed adding 2,300 jail beds within the next year as an emergency measure to deal with overcrowding brought on primarily by the rapid increase in the use of the cocaine derivative known as crack. Attorney General Edwin Meese, saying that crack has become a "crisis of epidemic proportions in some areas," has urged the creation of twenty-four special crack task forces around the country. Crack has emerged as the nation's number one drug problem, and New York is the crack capital.

I spent last weekend in the heart of that capital, Washington Heights, where addicts, former addicts, and the police agree that present efforts to stem the spread of crack and help its victims are ineffective.

Carlos, a thirty-six-year-old addict who looks fifty and is trying to wean himself from the drug, says dealers in as many as 1,500 apartments in Washington Heights (an area of forty square blocks) sell crack to users, mostly adults who drive into town in luxury automobiles from affluent areas in New Jersey and Westchester County. He says these users include businessmen and doctors, and some support a crack habit that costs up to $3,000 a day.

Ralph spent fifteen years as an addict, starting on heroin at the age of fifteen. He has been through several state rehabilitation programs, with varying degrees of short-term success. He says even the fear of AIDS was not strong enough to keep him out of a shooting gallery where many addicts shared the same needle.

Vince snorted cocaine for two and one half years and then began taking the drug intravenously.

What all of these men have in common, aside from their previous drug use, is that each is now clean or on his way to a drug-free life largely because of the work of one man, Tom Mahairas — himself a former drug user and a graduate of the hippie movement in the 1960s.

Mahairas saw that drug use, while having its roots in personality, family, and other problems, was primarily related to a spiritual dysfunction. After a life-transforming encounter with God, Mahairas became a preacher and established the Manhattan Bible Church to help people in the Harlem-Washington Heights area. In 1983 he also acquired a former orphanage in West Park, N.Y., about ninety minutes north of the city, where he established "Camp Transformation" for those who wanted to get off drugs, but who had no place to go.

Mahairas tells me that there is a six-month waiting period at virtually every government-supported detoxification center; too long a wait for a person who is seeking help now.

There are four objectives for those who come to Camp Transformation: to become totally drug-free; to obtain a high school equivalency diploma; to develop, through Biblical principles, qualities of purity, honesty, respect, and obedience; and to work with other young men to learn various skills.

The camp is taking thirty men this year and must turn away many more for lack of money. The cost to transform these lives is $3,600 per person, roughly what some addicts spend in a single day for their crack habits.

Captain Michael Mandel of the Thirty-Fourth Precinct believes Mahairas's program and others like it are needed if the crack epidemic is to be stopped. But Mandel says taxpayers apparently do not want to spend money on detoxification centers; they want more police, which alone cannot solve the problem.

It is not enough to lock up the dealers and users. The users must be helped so that they will not provide repeat business for the dealers.

Those who would shy away from a spiritually based solution to the crack problem need to ask themselves "What alternatives have proven to work better?" Carlos, Ralph, and Vince (and many others I spoke with) had all been through government-sponsored programs with limited or no success. At Camp Transformation, however, each man testifies to having attained control of his life.

Captain Mandel says some television programs like "Miami Vice" have "glamorized" drugs. "When you see crack," he says, "you associate it with affluence, fast cars, and the opposite sex. It makes you part of a group."

The former addicts I talked with say Mahairas's program has worked for them where all others have failed. They are part of a group, too, but perhaps they hear a different drumbeat.

Maybe government officials have been looking for answers in the wrong places. If they want to see a program that really works, they ought to visit the Greek preacher, Tom Mahairas, on 205th Street in New York City.

October 16, 1986

SEVENTY-TWO

THE "TRICKLE UP" THEORY

Systems are not made to be compassionate. People are.

For half a century, welfare has been a political football for conservative Republicans and a security blanket for liberal Democrats. Now, the Reagan Administration is proposing that the welfare system, be altered from a "trickle down" approach, under which the federal government dispenses billions of dollars from Washington, to a "trickle up" system, which would place state and local governments in control of much of the money.

According to the White House Low-Income Working Group of the Domestic Policy Council, the "trickle up" system would allow "policy ideas and implementation to percolate from the bottom up, to the federal government from the individuals, communities, and states that have to live with these policies."

Under the proposal, Congress would authorize the federal government to grant waivers permitting states to set up welfare experiments that deviate from federal laws and regulations.

In a report to the President, the Working Group says, "The system is composed of numerous and expensive programs, yet those programs have failed to lift many Americans out of poverty. The system should be compassionate, yet among recipients it inspires confusion and anger. The system makes a special effort to aid children, yet it provides little or no incentive for mothers and fathers to form and maintain self-reliant families. The system should encourage people to be self-sufficient, yet its incentives inspire passivity and undermine the desire to work."

As laudable as this effort to reform fifty years of welfare may be, there is one basic and, to my mind, serious flaw. The

Administration seeks to replace one system with another system, when it is the very idea of a system as the principal means of helping the poor out of their poverty that is the problem.

Systems are not made to be compassionate. People are. Systems do not give those on welfare a feeling of self-worth, hope, and meaning in life. People do.

The welfare system has undermined a primary responsibility for individuals to be their brothers' and sisters' keepers. The government has made it possible for many of us to feel no compassion or responsibility for the poor. Free to pursue pleasure and materialism, we now direct our energies to the acquisition of things and view aid to the poor and the homeless as a responsibility of government. After all, we reason, isn't that what taxes are for? So if there are poor and homeless people, it is a testimony to the failure of government programs or a lack of "compassion" by whoever is President rather than an indictment of our own self-centeredness.

Welfare reform needs to be broadened beyond the Reagan Administration's proposals. Government ought to be considering ways by which it can relinquish primary responsibility for the poor and return it as a privilege, not a burden, to churches, charities, civic groups, and individuals in local communities.

While it needs to make living on the dole unattractive, government also needs to make individual compassion for those hooked on the welfare drug more appealing.

The effect of welfare has been to remove the incentive of the haves to help the have-nots. It has taken away personal responsibility and replaced it with an easier to ignore institutional responsibility.

I have long been intrigued by a study conducted by a congressional office that showed that if every church and synagogue in America became responsible for only one family on public assistance, the welfare rolls would evaporate. Stated that way, eradication of poverty becomes a feasible goal. And why are these religious institutions receiving tax exemptions if not, in part, because they are expected to perform services beneficial to the nation, such as caring for poor people?

Tax exemption is a privilege, not a right. If individuals are required to justify their claims for tax deductions and exemptions, why shouldn't religious and civic groups be required to do the same if, as part of their reason for being, they are expected to help the poor?

Perhaps the federal government could supply every tax-exempt religious and civic organization with a list of welfare recipients living in their own community. It could then ask those institutions to help with the kind of assistance only a caring, compassionate group of individuals working and living in the same town can provide. Some are already offering such a service. Many more could. Those who refuse might be required to forfeit a percentage of their tax exemption, and the resulting funds could be shared by those exercising their responsibility.

It might be just what is needed to resuscitate the real heartbeat of America: compassion for the truly needy.

December 18, 1986

SEVENTY-THREE

REFORMING THE "CRIMINAL" JUSTICE SYSTEM

The federal and state prisons have succeeded only in creating a revolving door that is turning criminals back into society to commit new and often worse crimes.

The Justice Department says there are more people in prison in the United States than ever before, 528,945 inmates in federal and state institutions.

In California, which housed 10 percent of all the nation's prisoners at the end of 1985, Governor George Deukmejian recently called the legislature into special session to seek approval for a new state prison near downtown Los Angeles. The governor warned that current prison overcrowding could lead to a major "prison riot."

Forty-two states are under federal court orders to do something to alleviate prison overcrowding.

The federal and state prisons have succeeded only in creating a revolving door that is turning criminals back into society to commit new and often worse crimes.

Neither liberals, who have traditionally argued for more lenient probation policies but not a better rehabilitative plan, nor conservatives, who have favored tougher sentencing and more prisons, have proposed workable solutions to the crime problem and the high recidivism rate.

It is time to try a third way.

The Rand Corporation recently concluded a study titled

"Prison Versus Probation in California: Implications for Crime and Offender Recidivism."

The major finding of the study was that "imprisonment was associated with a higher probability of recidivism" than was probation. Shocking (to me) was the finding that 45 percent of those in the sample studied were in prison for property crimes. These nonviolent offenders shared quarters with murderers, rapists, robbers, and other violent felons.

According to the Justice Department, 16.1 percent of those sent to prison have no prior criminal record. For them, prison can be a training ground for a life óf often violent crime.

In Arizona, 61 percent of the inmates are serving their first prison term for nonviolent crimes.

Indiana discovered in a study commissioned in 1981 that 20 percent of its inmates were first offenders convicted of nonviolent crimes. The cost to the state for keeping them in prison was $20 million per year, not counting welfare payments to their dependents.

The Federal Bureau of Investigation says that 74 percent of those released from prison will be back within four years.

It costs an average of $17,324 annually to keep someone in prison. Building a new prison costs between $60,000 and $80,000 PER CELL. Over the next thirty years it will cost twelve and a half times that much, or $1 million per cell, to have it occupied. The total annual budget for state and federal prisons as of June 30, 1984, was $8.5 billion.

What to do?

In a new book, *Crime and its Victims* (Inter-Varsity Press), Daniel Van Ness, director of Justice Fellowship in Washington, D.C., makes a compelling case for restoring the concept of restitution to the criminal justice system, particularly for nonviolent offenders.

Van Ness says, "It is surprising to most people that early legal systems which form the foundation for Western Law emphasized the need for offenders and their families to settle with victims and their families. The offense was considered principally a violation against the victim and the victim's family. While the common welfare had been breached, and the community therefore had an interest and responsibility in seeing that the wrong was addressed and the offender punished, the offense was not considered primarily a crime against the state as it is today."

Van Ness says the United States has moved away from a rehabilitation model to a punishment model, which is not necessarily bad, but that we have equated prisons with punishment, which he says is wrong.

He says that making the offender accept responsibility is itself retribution and at the same time rehabilitative. "If this is done swiftly and with reasonable certainty, it will deter others from committing crimes and will deter the offender as well."

Every state has tried some alternative to imprisonment for nonviolent offenders. According to a Justice Fellowship study, thirty-two of the states report effective results, leading to reduced costs and/or a lower recidivism rate. These community-based restitution programs should be given every chance to succeed. Building more prisons clearly is no solution.

September 28, 1986

SEVENTY-FOUR

ONE TOOK THE STADIUMS, THE OTHER THE STREETS

On numerous occasions, Graham said his life was threatened because of his stand on race.

Not many people know of the relationship between Martin Luther King, Jr., and evangelist Billy Graham. Some would find even the suggestion of a relationship to be highly suspect. Yet, the two were friends.

I spent more than an hour with Graham recently, asking him to recall his own struggle with segregation, a struggle that brought the white evangelist from North Carolina into contact with the black Baptist preacher from Georgia for what turned out to be a few brief but shining moments.

Before their paths crossed, Graham said he took a firm stand against separate seating at his crusades for blacks and whites. The year was 1951. The city was Chattanooga, Tennessee.

The evangelist asked the ushers to take down ropes dividing the "white seats" up front from "black seats" in the back. When the ushers refused, Graham said he reached up and pulled the ropes down himself. Yet, because of the "racial conditioning" in the land, it would be three or four years before blacks would begin to feel comfortable mingling with whites at his meetings.

Then came the Montgomery boycott and Graham read of King's leadership role and invited the increasingly well-known preacher to address his team prior to a crusade in New York. King was asked to "tell us the position we ought to be taking," according to Graham. It was 1956.

It was during this period, Graham said, that the two became friends, King asking the young white preacher from North Carolina to call him "Mike," what he said his close friends called him.

In 1960, the two ministers flew together to Brazil for a meeting of the Baptist World Alliance. Graham held a dinner in King's honor, inviting 250 delegates from the Southern United States. He said that was easier to do in Brazil than it would have been in Jackson, Mississippi.

Graham said King brought a stirring message that offended no one and aroused the sympathy and understanding of the audience.

Graham would later tell King he did not feel the need to march with him, believing he could have a greater impact against segregation in his writings and by holding integrated meetings. He recalled the civil rights leader telling him, "That's okay. You take the stadiums and I'll take the streets." Graham later wrote a widely read article for the *Reader's Digest* called "The Most Segregated Hour in America."

On numerous occasions, Graham said his life was threatened because of his stand on race. The head of the "White People's Council" in one town vowed that Graham and his team would never get out of town alive. "But when the invitation was given [to repent of one's sin and commit his life to Christ], he was the first one down the aisle," said Graham.

During the racial troubles in Alabama in the early 1960s, President Lyndon Johnson called Graham and asked him whether he had guts enough to hold crusades throughout the state. He said he would. The Ku Klux Klan defaced Graham's banners and called him a communist (as they would later call King a Communist), but the crusades were wildly successful and although many towns were still divided, many others saw bridges of understanding built between black and white communities. King sent Graham a congratulatory telegram, which the evangelist still recalls with pleasure.

Graham remembered King telling an audience, "If it had not been for the work of Billy Graham in integrating his crusades in these big stadiums throughout the South, I could not have done the work I have been able to do."

Quite a testimony from a man who traveled on one road to a man who traveled on another, about a time when they met and grew to admire one another at an important intersection in the nation's history.

January 23, 1986

TRUTH AND OPPOSITION

TRUTH AND OPPOSITION

A woman in Towson, Maryland, wrote in response to a column I did on the importance of teaching chastity and fidelity as the best guarantee against AIDS and other unwanted consequences of too soon or the wrong kind of sex: "I'm sure you are going to get lots of hoots and maybe some hate mail for taking such an archaic stand. Well, I'm sure you didn't expect it to be easy swimming against the stream of 'If it feels good-do it'! It took a lot of courage and good self esteem to risk speaking the truth about chastity and fidelity after marriage. I congratulate you on your stand. Thank you for speaking out. Perhaps it will be a model for others who agree with you."

She was right. There were lots of hoots. And there was a bit of hate mail as well.

Most people recoil from opposition. Not me. I love it!

It is one of the yardsticks I use to determine whether I am speaking truth. People do not react pleasantly when they are challenged with something other than the prevailing world view. Truth causes confrontation.

So, when I write about homosexuality as being something other than normal, I am advised by a letter writer to "volunteer yourself for brain-trauma experiments, you sadistic creep!" That letter apparently was not written in the spirit of pluralism, tolerance, and freedom of thought we have come to expect from the liberal camp.

Neither was a tolerant spirit evident in a letter I received from an anonymous writer who called me first, "an ass," and then a "righteous ass." The latter I take to be some improvement over the former. At least the writer didn't call me a self-righteous ass, so there is hope.

Subjects involving religion seem to bring the humanistic termites in our culture out of the woodwork where they have been busily gnawing away at the foundations of this country. Wrote one of them from New York, "I was lucky. I saw religion for what it is, up there with the Easter Bunny and Santa Claus. I never fell into your trap. . . ."

Another New Yorker, apparently unaware of my six foot seven inch frame wrote, "If your feet are as big as your mouth, you shall be able to swallow *(sic)* them both after your stupid article."

Three things my parents taught me as a child: (1) Anyone can grow up to be president; (2) Cleanliness is next to godliness; (3) Liberals are tolerant of other people's views.

Imagine my surprise when I received a letter in response to one of my commentaries on National Public Radio, which reflected a rather intolerant view: "Carl (sic) Thomas's commentary . . . was the stupidest thing I've ever heard on the radio. . . . I was ashamed for you, to have to air junk like that."

Another letter to NPR was more direct. He thought I should be censored: "You simply have to replace commentator Cal Thomas with someone more enlightening."

A feminist writer in Illinois called me "a right-wing demagogue."

The point in sharing some of my "hate mail" (I've only included the "clean" ones) is to awaken the timid to the fact that speaking truth always brings opposition. In fact, it is one of the litmus tests, though not the only one, that proves one is headed in the right direction.

The late philosopher-theologian, Dr. Francis Schaeffer, whose writings strongly influenced my own thinking, spoke of what we can expect when we speak truth to a nation that is headed in another direction. In his, *How Should We Then Live?: The Rise and Decline of Western Thought and Culture*, Schaeffer noted that those who know the truth and have been set free by it must speak, in part to retard the growth of authoritarian government, which threatens our freedom and even our ability to speak truly in the future.

Said Schaeffer, "We are not excused from speaking, just because the culture and society no longer rest as much as they once did on Christian thinking. Moreover, Christians do not need to be in the majority to influence society.

"But we must be realistic. John the Baptist raised his voice, on the basis of Biblical absolutes, against the personification of power in the person of Herod, and it cost him his head. In the Roman Empire the Christians refused to worship Caesar along with Christ, and this was seen by those in power as disrupting the unity of the Empire; for many this was costly.

". . . No truly authoritarian government can tolerate those who have a real absolute by which to judge its arbitrary absolutes and who speak and act upon that absolute."

This is the tension point when it comes to court-imposed absolutes involving abortion, homosexual practice, surrogate mothers, affirmative action, and a host of other contemporary issues. It is also the tension point in geo-political affairs between those who recognize and accept the doctrine of evil and those who believe the Soviets can be made to behave if the United States simply says and does the right thing.

The absolutes that the liberal elite asks us to accept are not rooted in any foundation, save the shifting sand of their own fuzzy thinking. In fact, their very appeal to an absolute is itself illogical, since they have already rejected the concept of absolutes. Saying that absolute truth does not exist is an absolute statement.

So, opposition is a fact of life, for the soldier and for those who battle in the arena of ideas. This territory, be it in government, in academia, or in the media, will not be surrendered by those in power as it was during the bloodless coup that resulted in the deposing of our spiritual and intellectual forefathers and mothers. It must be taken back and the territory re-occupied.

It need not be a lonely battle. Those who fight it will, as the lady from Towson, Maryland, suggests, serve as a model for others who agree.

And there are some nice letters from people who are not content to sit idly by, including this one from a woman in the wonderfully named city of St. Paul: "I want to thank you so much for your courage, boldness, and truthfulness in your reporting despite horrendous opposition."

A Virginia man spoke the truth when he wrote, "A man is known not only by the company he keeps, but by the enemies he makes."

A seventy-four-year-old Pennsylvania man writes, "Congratulations on your work. If only we had more like you."

A few conservatives even listen to National Public Radio. One from Virginia wrote, "His thinking was refreshing and challenging; so much in contrast to the usual radio and TV commentary. Thank you for having him on your program. . . . Also, thank you for your courage."

So many favorable letter writers mention the word "courage" that it causes me to wonder why it should be considered courageous to say what is true. One would think that it would take more courage to promote falsehoods. Such is the condition of our culture.

I have never enjoyed any task in journalism as much as the one in which I am now involved. There is an internal affirmation that comes from speaking truth. In many ways it resembles my jumping off the high diving board for the first time. After a great deal of hesitancy, I wondered why I had never tried it before because the exhilaration was so great.

It is now time to replace timidity with boldness and to speak truth to a world that desperately needs something to believe in and someone of integrity to follow. As my newspaper publisher friend observed, "Everyone I know has run out of answers."

INDEX

COLOPHON

The typeface for the text of this book is *Baskerville*. Its creator, John Baskerville (1706-1775), broke with tradition to reflect in his type the rounder, yet more sharply cut lettering of eighteenth-century stone inscriptions and copy books. The type foreshadows modern design in such novel characteristics as the increase in contrast between thick and thin strokes and the shifting of stress from the diagonal to the vertical strokes. Realizing that this new style of letter would be most effective if cleanly printed on smooth paper with genuinely black ink, he built his own presses, developed a method of hot-pressing the printed sheet to a smooth, glossy finish, and experimented with special inks. However, Baskerville did not enter into general commercial use in England until 1923.

Substantive editing by George Grant
Copy editing by James B. Jordan
Cover design by Kent Puckett Associates, Atlanta, Georgia
Typography by Thoburn Press, Tyler, Texas
Printed and bound by R. R. Donnelley & Sons Company
Crawfordsville, Indiana